IDEAS UNITE, ISSUES DIVIDE

Peace & all good,

Rick Ryan

IDEAS
UNITE
ISSUES
DIVIDE

Essays on the Ethical Life

Richard Kyte

Piscator Books
LA CROSSE, WISCONSIN

Piscator Books
1900 Main Street
La Crosse, Wisconsin 54601

ideasunite.org

ISBN 10: 0-9816896-7-1
ISBN 13: 978-0-9816896-7-8

Library of Congress Card No. 2013947457

For Cindi

Contents

Contents

Contents

PREFACE

In September 2009 I met with Rusty Cunningham, publisher of the *La Crosse Tribune*, to discuss a proposal for a different kind of column. Would there be a place in the paper, I wondered, for a series of essays that used contemporary issues in the news as an occasion for exploring ideas?

It is not that I think there is anything wrong with the typical op-ed piece that urges readers to take a stand on the important political and societal issues of the day. It is important to be politically involved, and that means taking practical steps to see that good legislation is passed, that governmental agencies be held accountable, that citizens participate in elections, and so forth. But it is also important to understand the reasons for those practical steps, reasons that go well beyond the desire to cheer or boo for one's team. Indeed, understanding the reasons behind the positions is important precisely because it is the only way to find common ground on controversial issues.

Everything depends upon starting points. Yet, it seems to me, most of our public discussions consist of disputes about ending points without much attention to how we get there. Such disputes are often described as "ethical disputes," as if ethics consisted primarily of drawing the right conclusions. But that is a misleading, and rather recent, conception of ethics. The traditional conception of ethics is a picture of the good life from which the right choices follow as a matter of course.

The essays included in this volume, all of which have been published between October 2009 and June 2013 in the *La Crosse Tribune* in a series titled "The Ethical Life," are an attempt to explore some basic ideas that may help in navigating a common course through an increasingly complex and contentious world. Even people who are strongly divided by their opinions on controversial issues may be united in a shared commitment to basic ideas underlying their opinions.

I am grateful to Rusty Cunningham and the other members of the *La Crosse Tribune* editorial board—Chris Hardie, Scott Rada, and Mary Jo Werner—for providing the opportunity to contribute these pieces over the past four years and to Cindi Kyte, Tom Thibodeau, and Robert Schreur, who have improved them by patient reading and friendly criticism. I am also honored by the many readers who have asked that they be collected into a single volume.

July 2, 2013
Viterbo University
La Crosse, Wisconsin

IDEAS UNITE, ISSUES DIVIDE

CHARACTER

1. What Goes Around

A few weeks ago I walked out to my car and found a note placed under the windshield wiper. It read, "I accidentally scraped the side of your car. I'm so sorry. Just call me and I will pay for the repair." It was signed by one of the coaches where I work. It turned out not to be much of a scratch, but I was grateful for the incident because it gave me the opportunity to repay a favor from sixteen years ago.

I had just started a new job in Memphis. Hurrying into work one morning, I pulled into a parking spot and threw open my pickup door. It swung wide and left a long red scratch on the car parked next to me. The car belonged to Charlie Leonard, the men's basketball coach. I was worried about telling him: I was a new employee, and he was a well-known and respected figure on the campus; besides, I felt stupid for not being more careful. When I told him about it, he simply said, "Forget it. It's just a car; cars get dinged up."

Occasionally something like this occurs to remind us that there is a moral balance in the universe.

I can't count the number of times I've heard somebody explain a minor act of generosity or helpfulness by saying, simply, "What goes around, comes around." I've heard it used by someone explaining why he stopped to help a stranger change a flat tire, by another person saying why she gave a dollar to a needy person, or yet another person explaining why he volunteers each year to ring a bell for the Salvation Army.

On the face of it, this suggests belief in some kind of reciprocity, often called "karma." It is the notion that the laws of cause and effect operate according to a moral principle. If I give a dollar to you, someone will eventually give a dollar to me. If I help you change your flat tire, someone will eventually help me

3

change my flat tire. And sometimes that does in fact happen, but our actions are rarely returned in direct proportion. More often people believe that reciprocity is indirect: good actions result over time in good fortune and bad actions result in bad fortune.

But reciprocity may also be thought of simply as an expression of virtue. The generous person does not give a dollar to the homeless person because she thinks she may someday be homeless and need help herself; she gives it despite that possibility. The return on virtue is immediate, proportionate, and quite different from what is given. That is what is meant by "virtue is its own reward."

A virtue is a character trait, a habitual way of acting in certain contexts. But it is also a way of seeing things. To possess a virtue is to see possibilities for goodness in ordinary circumstances, in the same way that a musician can "see" music on a sheet of paper or a sculptor can "see" an emerging form in a lump of clay.

To the generous person, encountering someone in need is perceived as an opportunity to participate in, and enhance, a cycle of reciprocity that enhances one's life because it expands the bounds and the quality of one's relationships with others. By giving, I receive. Not the same thing that I give, but something else, and often unexpected: a friendship, an insight, a sense of being at home in the world. By contrast, the selfish person perceives every encounter with someone in need as a threat, an occasion for losing something. And by doing so he misses out on opportunities for living a richer life.

The expression, "What goes around, comes around," is more than just a belief that we will get something in return for our good deeds; it is an expression of how some people perceive the world at the moment of generosity, a perception of the world as a good place, in which each kind act imbues the world as a whole with more kindness. And by perceiving the world in that way, the generous person helps to make it so.

Sixteen years ago Charlie Leonard helped me to see the world differently. I may never have the chance to repay him directly, but I don't think that's what he was expecting anyway.

May 2, 2010

2. Happiness

What does happiness have to do with ethics?

Many people assume ethics is about what you have to do, not about what you want to do: it is a matter of "following the rules."

The typical family has over two-hundred rules applying to daily behavior inside the house—rules like, "Don't slam the door," "Turn off the light when you leave the bathroom," "Put your dirty clothes in the laundry basket." There are hundreds more rules for behavior outside the house—in the yard, in the car, at the grocery store, in a restaurant—and for special occasions, such as visiting relatives, going on a vacation or to a movie theater. Schools, of course, are notorious for the number of rules that they impose, and most workplaces are equally demanding, with some large corporations having layers upon layers of rules issuing from various departments, agencies, and governing bodies.

In the last thirty years or so, we have come increasingly to use the term "ethics" in the context of rules oversight and enforcement. Thus we have "ethics compliance officers" in many corporations, "ethics commissions" in federal, state, and local governments, health care "ethics committees" in hospitals, and "professional ethics committees" of the state bar associations. The list goes on and on. What they all have in common is the task of creating, implementing, and in some cases enforcing, rules and policies that have the effect of restricting people's freedom.

In a country whose founding documents claim that "life" and "liberty" are essential to the "pursuit of happiness," it is no wonder that so many people believe that happiness is irrelevant to—or even incompatible with—ethics.

This is why it is important to have a historical view of things. For at least two-thousand years, up until quite recently in our history, happiness was widely viewed as central to any robust understanding of the ethical life. This view goes back to Aristotle, who claimed that happiness was the "highest good," that is, the thing that everyone seeks, and the ultimate reason we do everything that we do. Of course, by "happiness," he didn't mean a temporary state of amusement or pleasure (such as you might get from watching a funny TV show or getting a new car); he meant a lasting and deep-seated condition, something we might refer to as "satisfaction" or "fulfillment."

Somewhere along the way, we started using the term "ethics" in place of what used to be called, more simply and directly, "rules," "regulations," "laws," "policies," "etiquette," or "civility."

There are a couple of dangers that come along with this change in language.

The first danger is a tendency to think that the only way to create a more ethical society (or organization, or family) is to put more rules in place. But in fact the opposite is true. An over-emphasis on rules corresponds to an under-emphasis on character. And it is character, not rules, that is at the heart of ethics. After all, as Plato observed, good people don't need rules to make them do what is right, and bad people will find ways around the rules. Of those who try to stop people from acting irresponsibly through legislation, he says, "they always think they'll find a way to put a stop to cheating on contracts and [so on], not realizing that they're really just cutting off a Hydra's head."

The second danger is that we will lose sight of the point of ethics and begin thinking that the various rules, regulations, and policies that authorities put in place are in themselves the determinants of right and wrong. But if we don't have a conception of ethics that goes beyond the "rules," how do we know when the rules themselves are unethical? How do find the words to express our sense that something we are required to do is not "right"?

As any child can attest, parents can have rules that are nonsensical, contradictory, or flat-out unfair. Bosses can implement rules that are counter-productive, self-serving, or even demeaning. And heaven knows, bureaucracies seem to specialize in the production of rules that at times appear designed to set-up obstacles in the way of citizens just trying to go about their business in their communities.

The reason that happiness is central to an understanding of ethics is that we need standards against which to evaluate whether our various activities—and the rules we put in place to govern our various activities—are genuinely "good" or merely arbitrary.

It may not be a standard we all agree upon—but that's a subject for another column.

January 31, 2010

3. Roots of Character

When the allies liberated Mauthausen on May 6, 1945, Martin Weiss found himself, along with a half dozen other Jewish survivors of the camp, walking out the gates and down the road, sick, malnourished, without possessions and with no idea where to go or what to do. They came across an overturned truck and searched it, finding a small tub of lard and an assortment of cow hides. They took the lard, and they took the hides, thinking they might be able to have some shoes made from the leather. None of them had shoes.

A little further down the road they saw a farmhouse. They knew that Germans lived inside. They regarded all Germans as Nazis, and they hated the Nazis for what they had done to them and their families. They were ready to kill any German they saw.

They walked up to the farmhouse and knocked on the door. When a woman answered they asked her for eggs and flour, which she gave them. Then they went to the barn, found a kettle, started a fire, and cooked some dumplings with the lard, eggs, and flour. After they finished eating, one of the men suggested they should take some of their hides and give them to the woman as payment for the food. Years later, Weiss reflected on that moment: "To this day I have a hard time understanding why we behaved so ethically. I could tell you it was because we were nice guys...baloney! We were mad. Yet, without any discussion, we all agreed to do the same thing."

This story illustrates the significance of character. The survivors didn't believe they owed the German woman anything. In fact, they believed that all Germans owed them a debt greater than could be repaid, and yet, faced with a particular situation in which they had asked for something and received it, they responded the way they had been brought up to respond, by paying the woman for what she had given them.

Character does not conform itself to our beliefs. It is deeper than that. It is formed through repeated actions, often beginning at a very young age, until the behaviors become habits, and the habits shape the very way in which we perceive ourselves and others. Aristotle called character our "second nature." It is not who we are born to be, or even who we wish to be, but who we become over time.

Character is not necessarily good. It consists of virtues, which are positive traits, and vices, which are negative traits. Virtues are regarded as positive because they tend to lead to happiness, at least in the long run. Vices lead to unhappiness in the long run, though they are often thought to be positive in the short run.

In western culture there are seven "classical" virtues, each with corresponding vices: four cardinal virtues (justice, wisdom, courage, and moderation) and three theological virtues (faith, hope, and love).

It is interesting to note that we tend to speak of "values" rather than "virtues" when talking about ethical traits. But the term "value" was imported into ethics fairly recently from the field of economics. "Value" is a term implying relative worth whereas "virtue" refers to a behavioral trait. My used car has value—whatever someone is willing to pay for it. But courage, or justice, or moderation are not values; they are ways of perceiving and acting in various situations.

Values language has become popular because it is fairly easy for most of us to say what we value. It is what we believe to be important. The problem is, we often don't act according to our values. We act according to our virtues and vices—according to the traits that have become part of who we are, through our habits and upbringing. Martin Weiss didn't value the Germans after he was liberated. But he still acted with justice, despite the injustice done to him, because that's the kind of person he had become.

At the time of year when we naturally turn to a reassessment of our lives, bringing new energy and enthusiasm to becoming better selves, it's good to remember that the only way to change our character is through the repeated actions that turn into habits. There is no short-cut to virtue.

January 2, 2011

4. CARDINAL VIRTUES

The cardinal virtues (named after the Latin word *cardes*, or "hinge") have been considered the pivotal characteristics of human flourishing since classical Greece.

Plato's *Republic* provides the first thorough argument for the significance of the four virtues, claiming that justice, both for individuals and societies, proceeds from the harmony of mind, body, and spirit, and that harmony is achieved when each of the three parts of the person achieves excellence in its respective functioning. The excellence ("virtue") of the mind is wisdom, the excellence of the body is temperance, and the excellence of the spirit is courage.

Virtues lead to happiness because they allow one to have deeper, more meaningful relationships with other people. However, they also make one more vulnerable to unhappiness for the very same reason. Only the person who has a deep friendship can experience the sorrow of the loss of a friend. Only a person who cares deeply about something can feel the despair of loss.

Consider the classic Frank Capra film *It's a Wonderful Life*. The film covers the life of George Bailey, depicting him as a virtuous person: he is brave (he saves his brother from drowning in a pond); he is prudent (he saves a woman who is issued a wrong prescription by using his own judgment); he is moderate in his habits (he turns down opportunities for wealth, lives in an old house, and is generous to others). But near the end of the film, George considers taking his life because he despairs: he is facing prison because of an apparent misuse of funds at his Building and Loan Company; he thinks that his life amounts to nothing.

George is saved by the interference of an angel, who gives

him a vision of what the community of Bedford Falls would have been like if he had never lived. He is also saved by his family and friends, who, in the final scene, come to his aid, assuring him that he is loved and that they will help him out of his financial troubles.

The other principal character in the film is Mr. Potter, a thoroughly bad person. He is greedy, insensitive, and ill-tempered. When things do not go according to his plans, he gets angry and plots revenge. But this is the crucial point: he never despairs. Only the good person despairs, because he cares deeply; Mr. Potter cannot despair because he cannot lose anything he really cares about.

Mr. Potter would say that he is happier than George, but part of what happens to people when they acquire character traits is that their conception of happiness changes. Mr. Potter has become incapable of recognizing true happiness. It always seems like something else to him—foolishness, naïveté, lack of ambition, or, in his own words, "sentimental hogwash."

This peculiar feature of virtues and vices makes them problematic: those who possess the virtues, know that they are virtues. People who have the vices disagree; they tend to think the virtues are vices. The only way to really see who is right and who is wrong in the debate is to see what becomes of people who exhibit the different character traits.

January 16, 2011

5. COURAGE

Of the four cardinal virtues, courage is the most readily recognized in contemporary Western societies. The fact that we still employ the concept on a regular basis indicates that it is widely valued and praised. But even though we praise courage, we are increasingly becoming a society that does everything it can to prevent children from developing it.

Richard Louv, author of *Last Child in the Woods*, documents the widespread societal shift away from outdoor play. One of the reasons for the shift is, of course, the increasing popularity of electronic media. But another factor is parents' preoccupation with children's safety and the perception that nature is unsafe.

Virtues are developed incrementally by facing situations in which they may be expressed. In the case of courage, this means that facing one's fears and learning how to overcome them is necessary for acquiring the virtue.

For generations of children, playing outdoors provided the chief opportunities for facing fearful situations and learning how to act in spite of those fears. Sleeping outdoors at night, hearing strange sounds, imagining a bear prowling the woods, hearing thunder, seeing lightning strike, finding a snake on a path, removing a leech from one's leg, getting lost on a hike— all are occasions for fear, and, more importantly, occasions for developing courage by learning how to overcome fear.

We can learn something from first-person accounts of heroic actions. An example is the "Miracle on the Hudson" in which Captain Chesley "Sully" Sullenberger successfully landed US Airways Flight 1549 on the Hudson River after losing both engines shortly after takeoff. He was rightly hailed as a national hero for saving the lives of 155 passengers and crew.

When asked afterwards about what he was thinking during the crisis, he talked about mundane things: going through the steps to try to restart the engines, calculating the speed and altitude required to turn back to LaGuardia, then deciding to glide the plane to a landing on the river. He was well aware of the urgency. He said, "the physiological reaction I had to this was strong, and I had to force myself to use my training and force calm on the situation." Yet because he had many years of flight experience and had trained for emergency situations, he was able to focus on the task at hand and not be distracted by fears of what could go wrong. Sully was not born brave; he learned how to be brave through years of practice.

Courage may be required whenever one has to face some kind of danger. And because there are many kinds of danger, there are many occasions for courage in one's life. Physical injury is one kind of danger, but loss of work, money, affection, or reputation are also dangers that may require courage. A child standing up to a bully at school, an employee reporting an ethics violation at work, a politician taking an unpopular stand on an issue, a friend asking forgiveness for a betrayal: all require varying degrees of courage.

Parents' responsibilities extend not only to keeping their children safe but also to ensuring they have opportunities to mature intellectually and emotionally. That requires regular exposure to the fearful so that children develop the ability, as Sully puts it, to "force calm on the situation."

Paradoxically, this is the only way to ensure our children's safety in the long run, for, as Louv points out, "a case can be made that we endanger our children by separating them too much from nature, and that the reverse is also true—that we make them safer, now and in the future, by exposing them to nature."

A society that values courage must pay attention to how its children are being raised, ensuring that opportunities for encountering and overcoming the fearful are as plentiful as opportunities for reading, writing, playing music, throwing a football, dancing, and watching TV. There must be room for making one's way through the unanticipated complexities of the unconstructed world.

February 13, 2011

6. Temperance

In 1776 an event occurred that set the course for the American way of life: Adam Smith's *The Wealth of Nations* was published. So influential did Smith's ideas become to the burgeoning American republic that one could almost consider the Scottish philosopher to be among the nation's founders.

Smith established a blueprint and a justification for free market economies. He argued that the common good is advanced most effectively by giving individuals the freedom to pursue their own interests: "every individual...intends only his own gain, and he is...led by an invisible hand to promote an end which was no part of his intention." In other words, people are selfish, but if they are allowed to act on their selfishness, they will inadvertently promote the common good.

Smith was not oblivious to the potential dangers of his proposal. One concern arises from the division of labor. In primitive societies, he said, every person assumes many roles, which naturally lends itself to a shared conception of the public good. But in a capitalistic society, the division of labor requires that each person becomes a specialist and spends much of his or her life doing only one thing. This leads to a narrowness of view, and thus to bitter political disputes defined by special interests.

Another concern arises from the conflation of needs and desires. In a capitalistic society the consumption of goods drives the economic engine. It doesn't matter much whether the goods are necessary or not, what's important is that people keep producing and consuming them. This produces an inclination for people to think that they cannot be satisfied without "more." And since there is no end to "more," there is no reaching a state of satisfaction.

The remedy for the first problem, Smith said, is public education. Society needs education to provide citizens with a broad perspective and a common language so that political disputes may be negotiated reasonably and effectively.

The remedy for the second problem is to cultivate the virtue of temperance, so that people do not become slaves to the very desires that generate the wealth of the economy.

Temperance, one of the four cardinal virtues, had been a fixture in western societies since the ancient Greeks. It consisted in the ability to regulate one's desires, taking the appropriate kind of enjoyment in physical pleasures. The temperate person was able to distinguish needs from desires and not allow reason to be swayed by lust or gluttony.

Among ancient writers an oft-cited example of intemperance was Philoxenenus of Leucas, a famous glutton, who wished to have a neck as long as a crane's so that the pleasure of swallowing his food could be extended indefinitely. Nobody today wishes to have a neck as long as a crane, but plenty of people will buy diet soda, or fat-free potato chips, or Viagra, in order to extend the pleasures of drinking, eating, and sex indefinitely and without (apparent) consequence.

In today's society, the management of pleasure has come to be seen not as a moral problem but as a technological challenge. The very word "temperance" is nearly extinct from our everyday vocabulary, a sure indication that we have little use for the concept.

Reflecting on the growing intemperance of his age, the English poet William Wordsworth wrote:

The world is too much with us; late and soon,
Getting and spending, we lay waste our powers;
Little we see in Nature that is ours;
We have given our hearts away, a sordid boon!

If Wordsworth thought the citizens of 19th century England were out of tune with nature, wasting their powers by "getting and spending," what would he say of Americans today? What would Adam Smith say of a people who extol the material advantages of a free market while failing to appreciate its moral risks?

February 27, 2011

7. Justice

At a recent town hall meeting on the topic of criminal justice, Judge Ramona Gonzalez made a simple yet profound observation regarding the inmates of the newly expanded county jail. "The people who are in jail," she explained, "are your neighbors; they are the people who live and work among you." The observation is simple because it is obviously true; it is profound because it raises a question about the very nature of justice.

Most people think of justice as a system of laws and institutions designed to maintain the social contract. The guiding metaphor is balance, established by law and restored through punishment, symbolized by a blindfolded woman holding a scale.

But another way of thinking about justice is not as a system but as a virtue, that is, a character trait embodied in people and communities. Plato regarded justice as the greatest of the four cardinal virtues, because it incorporates the other three. To be just, he insisted, requires good judgment (wisdom), sacrifice (temperance), and a willingness to take risks (courage). It consists of living in right relationship with others.

One of the risks of thinking of justice in terms of a system of balance maintained by the state is that the goal is never fully achieved. This naturally leads to resentment among those who are unable to achieve fair treatment under the laws.

An example is provided in *Michael Kohlhaas,* a novella by the 19th century German writer Heinrich von Kleist. The story is about a man whose horses are illegally seized by a nobleman. Kohlhaas's efforts to get his horses returned to him are met with indifference by government officials, so he resorts to violence, declaring himself an outcast, no longer bound by the laws of civil society. "I call that man an outcast who is denied the protection of the laws!" Kohlhaas declares. "For I need this protection if my peaceful calling is to prosper;...and whoever denies me it thrusts me out among the beasts of the wilderness." Kohlhaas leads an armed revolution that accomplishes his original aim: his horses are restored to him. But, in the end, he is executed for crimes committed in the course of seeking justice.

A story illustrating the other way of thinking about justice is told in the Gospel of Luke. A lawyer, wanting to know the precise extent of his obligations under the Torah commandment to "love your neighbor as yourself," asks Jesus, "Who is my neighbor?" Instead of responding with a definition of "neighbor," Jesus tells the parable of the Good Samaritan and then asks the lawyer, "Which of these three, do you think, was neighbor to the man who fell into the hands of the robbers?"

By telling a story instead of giving a definition, Jesus turns the burden of defining justice back onto the lawyer. Loving one's neighbor may be required by the law, but the law itself is properly understood only by those who are able to perceive the stranger as neighbor. The Samaritan, despite being an outcast, acts upon an understanding of right relationship that stands under, and therefore informs, the law.

Kohlhaas declared himself an outcast, a person without obligation under the law, because the law failed to protect his rights; the Samaritan, also an outcast, nevertheless took upon himself an obligation that the law did not specifically require.

Those who have broken society's laws do not thereby cease being our neighbors. Nor can any of us cease being a neighbor to others because society has disappointed our legitimate expectations.

That is why it is important to acknowledge that the people who are inmates in the county jail are not outcasts but neighbors, an idea you will not find written in the Wisconsin stat-

utes, but may find written in the hearts of those who have acquired the virtue of justice.

March 13, 2011

8. Hope

In 1991 I was a graduate student at Johns Hopkins University, six years into a program that was supposed to take four years. Completing the dissertation still seemed years away, and job prospects in my field looked bleak. Walking into the office of my advisor, an atheist philosopher from New York and perhaps the most cynical person I'd ever met, I gave voice to my despair. He interrupted me: "I thought you Christians regarded hope as a virtue."

His words shocked me. I had never thought of hope as a virtue, that is, as a character trait that can be cultivated by the things we pay attention to, the actions we undertake, and the words we use. Instead, I had assumed hope and despair were simply conditions one fell into, emotional responses to situations and largely outside of one's control.

I should have known better, for as soon as one begins paying attention to people, it is obvious that those who are hopeful are, as a general rule, no better off than those who are in the habit of complaining about things. It's just that they see things differently, and that leads them to respond to situations and other people more positively.

My grandmother was a person of hope. She took to heart Paul's assurance in his Letter to the Romans that "all things work together for good for those who love God." This is a difficult passage if interpreted to mean that all one's dreams will be realized. My grandmother's dreams were certainly not realized, but she did not allow the disappointments to define her life.

She confirmed by example the distinction I learned much later, that hope is not the same as optimism. Hope is the conviction that things will turn out well in the end, but optimism is the idea that one's plans will work out as expected. It is optimistic to think that I will win the lottery; it is hopeful to be assured that, whether I win the lottery or not, things will nevertheless turn out well.

My grandmother's hope found expression in loving service to others. She knew that love of God must be practically expressed through acts of hospitality. She delighted in holidays, which provided the opportunity to entertain guests. And she was attentive to rituals, regarding them as gifts from generations past, providing forms of social interaction which could be modified and adapted, but never abandoned. Over the years this had resulted in a life rich in relationships, though poor in material goods.

In speaking to young people today I find a great deal of anxiety about the future. And they have much to concern them: environmental degradation, global warming, nuclear meltdowns, economic recession, war. But mainly they worry about stepping into a world of mean-spiritedness, in which those in charge don't care enough about them to ensure that they will have a welcome role in society.

It seems to me that our chief responsibility to young people is not to engage in a politics of despair, but to hold onto the forms of conduct that allow civil society to flourish: respect in the ways we address one another; truthfulness in words and actions; and a sincere commitment to the common good.

Whenever we treat one another with incivility because we are more concerned with obtaining immediate goals than preserving the integrity of relationships, we deprive our children of the hope that is their proper inheritance.

Shortly before my grandmother passed away, she discussed her funeral arrangements. Her chief concern was leaving enough money to provide a good meal after the ceremony. And then she instructed, "Be sure to have white linen on the tables."

She didn't want her final guests to think she didn't care about them.

April 10, 2011

9. Love

Is there such a thing as the "greatest good," something that everyone desires and that is the ultimate goal of all our actions? Aristotle thought so, and many philosophers since have agreed with him. The "greatest good," he claimed, is happiness.

What is this happiness that everyone desires, but which is so hard to specify with precision? That's where the difficulty comes in. Perhaps we all agree that we desire happiness, but each of us is made happy by different things.

Well, maybe not. It's easy to say that we all have different ideas about happiness. That's certainly true. But does it follow that different things make us happy?

In one respect, yes. One person enjoys golfing and another enjoys video games. One person enjoys painting and another enjoys music.

But even of the activities that we take special pleasure in, we often find that we aren't very good judges. The person who can't wait until retirement so that he can fish every day discovers that while fishing two days a week is great fun, fishing six days a week is as burdensome as work, and the loss of his work deprived him of the daily companions he used to talk to about fishing.

What we think will make us happy and what actually does make us happy are two different things. That's why sayings such as "The grass is always greener on the other side of the fence" and "Be careful what you wish for, you may receive it" are so popular. They remind us that our perceptions are unreliable.

Each of us has been mistaken at times about what we wanted, or thought we wanted. As we age, we accumulate regrets: things we wish we had done, or done differently, or not done at all. And this may lead to a kind of wisdom over time, an ability to discern lasting satisfaction from ephemeral pleasure.

What wisdom teaches is that genuine happiness comes from the capacity for love; every other source of pleasure is limited and limiting.

This lesson is obscured by superficial depictions of love in popular culture—in movies, television dramas, and music. They easily lead us into two common errors: that love is a commodity or an event.

If we think of love merely as the satisfaction of physical desire, we are thinking of it as a commodity, something that can be purchased and possessed. The range here is vast, from pornography and prostitution to earrings and chocolate. Not that there is anything wrong with earrings themselves, but thinking of them as the object of love is problematic because anything that can be possessed can provide at most a temporary spike in the level of pleasure that one experiences. And that doesn't provide lasting happiness.

The other common error is thinking about love as something that happens to me, like "falling in love," rather than something I do. Emotional attraction is something that happens to us, of course, and its workings are mysterious. But it is through the process of deepening the relationship that we discover the potential for deep and lasting friendship with another person. Emotional attraction is just the doorway we pass through, it is not the destination. If the feeling of "falling in love" is what you want to make permanent, you are bound to be disappointed. You can't just stand in the doorway forever.

Genuine happiness comes from developing the capacity to have direct concern for the well-being of others. This is love. It is an expansion of the self, so that who I am is not limited by the reach of my arms or the extent of my possessions. I am born mere potential. I become who I am in the fullness of my relationships with others. It is literally true, and not just a clever saying, that when I love another, I double myself.

Developing the capacity for love does not guarantee a life of happiness at all moments. Paradoxically, the more we love others, the more we open ourselves up to sorrow. When we lose someone we love, we lose a part of ourselves—not the self that we were when we were born, but part of the greater self we became when we began to love.

In the self that remains we retain not only the memory of those we have lost, but hold the promise of those who will need our love tomorrow.

February 21, 2010

10. ANGER

My grandpa Emmett was a passionate fan of pro wrestling. He had no doubts about the integrity of the sport and would express indignation if anyone suggested that the matches were rigged. One night at the Fargo Coliseum, he was so outraged by the referee's failure to keep the "bad guys" from cheating, that he took matters into his own hands. He grabbed a cane from the old man sitting next to him, snuck up behind Larry "Pretty Boy" Hennig, and whacked him on the head. In the furor that ensued, he managed to escape back to his seat without getting nabbed by the security guards. But I was not so fortunate. My dad read about the incident in the newspaper the next day and decided pro wrestling matches were unsuitable for 10 year olds. I was banned for life.

Anger is a dangerous and unpredictable emotion. The old expression "to fly off the handle" refers to how an axe head sometimes comes loose from the shaft at the top of the swing, causing harm to anyone who happens to be in the path of the flying projectile.

Like guilt, shame, resentment, indignation, and pride, anger is always accompanied by some kind of moral judgment. One cannot be angry at someone and also believe them to be in the right. But unlike the other moral emotions, its intensity is out of all proportion to the significance of the event that prompts it, and that makes it likely to be both personally and socially disruptive.

The Greek and Roman Stoics thought anger could be managed by learning how to control one's thoughts. Epictetus said that "what upsets people is not things themselves but their judgments about the things." This is useful advice because in our anger we can become obsessive and narrowly focused, neglecting to take into account relevant information and the broader context of a situation.

But sometimes anger is an appropriate response. All kinds of things happen in the world that we should feel angry about, such as racial discrimination, child exploitation, animal abuse, environmental degradation, and political corruption. Yet unless we are closely involved or can imagine some personal connection, we tend not to feel angry despite our judgment about it. Somebody inadvertently cutting me off on the Interstate is more likely to provoke an angry response than a dictator who murders innocent children in a foreign country.

Emerson calls this partiality—this inability to align our passion and our judgment with what is really going on in the world—the most "unhandsome part of our condition."

If only we could manage to express outrage at the people who really deserve it, for what they have actually done wrong, the world would be a much better place. And our lives would have more integrity.

One of the reasons we find prophets like Nathan, Amos, and Martin Luther King, Jr. inspiring is that they combine passion with a sense of justice. Their moral outrage is directed towards abuses of power that harm the innocent. When a person's emotions are in line with sound judgment, their very presence causes us to feel viscerally connected to a purpose greater than mere self-interest. By sharing in their indignation we find a measure of redemption.

But the prophets are exhausting. It takes a great deal of energy to sustain a genuine and passionate fight against injustice, so most of us settle for mild disapproval interrupted by the occasional outburst.

I don't know the real sources of my grandpa's rage, but I suspect it had little to do with Larry "Pretty Boy" Hennig. He just happened to be a convenient target. But I learned an important lesson that evening in the Fargo Coliseum. Anger is a powerful motivator, and it can lead one to take action when everyone else is content to sit along the sidelines jeering and complaining.

The great challenge is to make sure one's anger is appropriately directed, aligned with sound judgment rather than self-regard or misperception. No matter how good it feels at the time, you just can't go around hitting people over the head with a cane.

February 12, 2012

11. Forgiveness

It's curious that most ethics textbooks pay little, if any, attention to the topic of forgiveness.

In some ways that's understandable, because for the past two-hundred years ethics in Western societies has been dominated by the conviction that ethics is a matter of "doing the right thing," and that requires a nearly exclusive focus on figuring out some method for determining what the "right thing" is in a variety of complex situations.

But for at least two-thousand years before that, ethics was thought of more comprehensively, not only as the "right thing" to do, but also as the right way of doing things, which requires attention to the quality of our relationships. The very term "ethics" comes to us from the ancient Greeks, who evaluated all actions in light of the character traits that produced them. An action was considered to be "good" or "right," not because of its consequences, but because it was, for instance, "courageous," or "wise," or "reverent."

As the political philosopher Hannah Arendt noted, the two practices necessary for any society to sustain itself are promising and forgiving. Promising is the way in which we establish cooperation, whether that be political (in the form of laws), commercial (in the form of contracts), or personal (in the form of vows). But forgiving is needed because we invariably fail to keep our promises, and so it is necessary to continually repair our fractured relationships and restore our faith in one another so that we can go on living and working together.

One of the difficulties in talking about forgiveness as an ethical matter is that we tend to think of it too narrowly, as a specifically religious concept, for example, or perhaps as a psychological function, one of a variety of emotional responses to injury. We tend to equate it with "letting go" or "getting over" or "moving on," as if it were a matter a skillfully managing one's feelings for the purpose of emotional health. And while forgiveness is certainly important for emotional health, it defeats its own purpose if done solely for personal reasons. In order to really forgive you, I must do it for your sake (or ours).

I would like to suggest that we think of forgiveness in broad terms, covering all attempts to repair or restore broken relationships, ranging from minor personal injuries to major societal injustices. Forgiveness may then include not only the act of apologizing (or accepting an apology) for a personal insult, but also such things as inviting an estranged neighbor to dinner, asking a coworker for advice, giving a supplier another chance to fulfill the terms of a contract, making a speech at a battle site.

Forgiveness, conceived broadly, is central to ethics because maintaining good relationships with others is, or should be, the central focus of our lives. Unless we practice forgiveness on a regular basis, it is nearly impossible to maintain relationships in ways that allow our lives together to flourish. And lives that don't flourish together don't flourish at all.

April 4, 2010

12. GRATITUDE

My grandmother had a picture hanging in her dining room: an old man in prayer, a bowl of soup and loaf of bread in front of him, his reading glasses folded over a Bible.

Titled "Grace," it was a colored print of a photograph taken by Eric Enstrom in his Bovey, Minnesota studio in 1918. Thousands have been sold all over the world. In 2002 it was designated the official state photograph of Minnesota.

Asked what motivated the photo, Enstrom said: "I wanted to take a picture that would show people that even though they had to do without many things because of the war, they still had much to be thankful for."

Gratitude rarely makes anyone's list of the top virtues. Neither Plato nor Aristotle give it more than passing mention. Augustine speaks of divine grace but not the human response of gratefulness. Aquinas regards gratitude as a passive emotion resulting from acknowledging indebtedness. Even Ben Franklin neglects to include it in his list of thirteen.

Only Cicero, among the classical writers, gives it much thought, and he elevates it above all others: "There is nothing which I can esteem more highly than being and appearing grateful, for this one virtue is not only the greatest, but is also the parent of all the other virtues."

Cicero argues that gratitude is at the root of patriotism, love of parents, wisdom, kindness, and friendship, for each of these qualities requires a grateful heart. Implicit in his claim is the idea that gratitude cannot simply be something we feel, but an attitude we cultivate, for virtues are not mere feelings; they are traits of character, and traits of character result from action.

Recent research supports Cicero's elevation of gratitude as one of the chief virtues.

Reviewing empirical research on the sources of happiness, psychologists Emily Polak and Mike McCullough found that gratitude is actually much more closely linked to happiness than is material prosperity. They write, "The pursuit of wealth and possessions as an end unto itself is associated with lower levels of well-being, lower life satisfaction and happiness, more symptoms of depression and anxiety, more physical problems such as headaches, and a variety of mental disorders."

Of course, well-being does require the satisfaction of basic material needs, such as food, health, shelter, and security, but the attempt to continually improve one's prospects in the world through material gain, rather than appreciating what one already has, proves to be counter-productive.

A common misconception is that gratitude is simply an emotional response to good fortune. But nothing could be further from the truth. Nearly everyone carries a cup of sorrow, some heavy burden that they do not share publicly, but which is present nevertheless, always just below the surface of daily interaction. Gratitude makes such burdens bearable.

When Holocaust survivor Nesse Godin spoke several years ago in La Crosse, some people were surprised by her joy, her sense of humor, the broad smile which seemed a permanent expression on her face. After her talk, someone asked how she could be so cheerful after the hardships and terrible losses she had endured. She replied, "Today I am with you, and I am so grateful to be in your presence and among such good people, but tonight I will go back to my room, and the nightmares will return."

For Nesse, like so many others, gratitude is not denial, nor is it the product of naïve optimism; it is a deliberate choice to acknowledge the goodness that is always present somewhere, no matter how fragile or tenuous it may seem at times.

After my grandmother died I asked about the picture of

the old man at prayer, but nobody seemed to know what had happened to it. Then a few years ago we found one at a garage sale. It hangs in our house now, and when I pass by it, I think of the hardships she endured—losing an infant son, caring for a spouse ravaged by stroke, living in an old school bus during the depression. And I think of the last years of her life, living alone, with diabetes and a weak heart, volunteering at the local nursing home, and I hear her saying, "Count your blessings."

December 2, 2012

13. POWER

Lord Acton, the nineteenth century British historian, famously said: "Power tends to corrupt, and absolute power corrupts absolutely. Great men are almost always bad men."

The idea that power is a corrupting influence has a long history. Yet, in and of itself, power is a good thing. It is the ability to get things done. It can take many forms: strength, intelligence, persistence, wealth, cleverness, reputation, experience. But it can be harmful to the people who are subjected to the effects of power, if it is used without their consent. And it may also be harmful to the person who wields it, particularly if it allows one to evade the social consequences of bad behavior.

In the *Republic* Plato tells the story of a shepherd named Gyges who found a magic ring. He discovered that when he put the ring on his finger he would turn invisible. So he put on the ring, went to the royal court, seduced the queen, killed the king, and took over the kingdom. Then Plato posed the question: if two people, one who is just and the other who is unjust, each found magic rings, would they both end up acting in the same way?

That's a hard question to answer. We don't have any magic rings lying around to do an experiment. But we do have examples of many people—movie stars, athletes, politicians, entrepreneurs—who have risen from humble origins to positions of wealth and prestige. And many of them have acted despicably. The news media is replete with stories of powerful people behaving irresponsibly: Tiger Woods, Roman Polanski, Michael Vick, Kenneth Lay, Bill Clinton, Bernard Madoff, Martha Stewart, Mark Sanford—and most recently, Brett Favre.

If your entire life has been defined by your success at climbing the ladder, what do you do when you get to the top rung? Experience shows that most people either go back down to help others up—or they just fall off.

Joe Magee, an assistant professor of management at New York University, has been doing interesting research lately on the psychology of power. One of the things he discovered is that people in high power positions tend not to take into account the perspective of other people, whereas people in low power positions tend to pay more attention to the perceptions and attitudes of others. Powerful people literally see the world differently than others do. Maybe that's why powerful people so often seem to be blind-sided by the magnitude of the scandal when they get caught doing something wrong. They really don't seem to have considered how their actions appear to others.

Fortunately, we also have many examples of people in power who appear to be decent citizens: Donald Driver, Kevin Garnett, Oprah Winfrey, Bill Gates, Barbara Bush, Jimmy Carter, and Elie Wiesel are a few who come to mind. These are people who, on the whole, seem to have done a good job of retaining perspective. Their focus is outwards: on their teammates, their clients, their colleagues, their fellow citizens.

People who are successful at managing power without having it negatively affect their character do so by placing certain restrictions on their lives so that they have to remain accountable for their behavior. They establish and maintain relationships with people they can trust, people who know what they are doing and who will tell them the truth, people who aren't afraid to criticize them when necessary, to take them down a notch.

This is known as humility.

When you have no power, humility is forced upon you. But when do you have power, you have to work extra hard to maintain humility, so that you don't delude yourself into thinking you are invincible.

October 24, 2010

14. REVENGE

There are evenings when I am so tired of being nice to people all day that all I want to do is sit down in front of the television with a can of La Crosse Lager and watch a Dirty Harry movie. Actually, just about any revenge movie will do, as long as it follows the formula: in the beginning some innocent person is injured or killed, the hero seeks justice, he has his life threatened in a variety of ways, and in the end he kills the bad guy.

For the revenge formula to work, the viewer has to identify with the hero and take pleasure in the violent dispatch of the villain. And in order to take pleasure in the violence, the viewer must come to see the villain as irredeemably wicked, so that he is seen to deserve a painful death.

In the final scene of *The Enforcer,* Harry Callahan blows the bad guy up with a bazooka. Just before the explosion the director cuts to a close-up of the villain's face, eyes wide and mouth agape as he watches Harry point the bazooka in his direction. This is the crucial scene of the revenge movie: the villain sees his violent end approaching. He looks his killer in the eyes. In the convention of movie making, this means he looks us (the audience) in the eyes. We are the ones who carry out the vengeance.

The German language has a word for the kind of emotion at work in situations like this: *schadenfreude.* It means, literally, "damage-joy"—taking pleasure in another's pain.

Most westerns follow the revenge formula, though curiously, some of the best westerns do not, like *Red River* and *Fort Apache.* Others, like *The Searchers, The Man Who Shot Liberty Valance,* and *Unforgiven* are great because they both rely upon and call into question the revenge formula. *(Gran Torino* is a recent movie of this type, using the revenge formula while raising questions about it.)

One justification for this kind of film is based on the idea of catharsis, that negative emotions need purging, and it is better to purge them in a fantasy than to take out one's unreleased frustrations on real people. There is something to that. There is a sense of relief that comes from expressing negative emotions, and that expression can take many forms, including the exercise of imagination. In ancient Greece, audiences would attend a play by Sophocles; now we go to a movie by Mel Gibson.

But there is a worry that taking pleasure in revenge movies may become habitual, because taking pleasure in something repeatedly shapes our very perception of things, so that we may come gradually to see more and more people as fitting into the exceptional category of deserving violent suffering.

In America we prize our freedoms more than anything. We don't like people telling us what we can or cannot do. The acid test for the legitimacy of any activity is: does it hurt anyone else? But what if by watching such movies I hurt myself? And what if in hurting myself I become less than I could be as a father, a husband, a friend, a neighbor, and a citizen?

It is our great privilege as moral beings to be self-formative, not only to be a certain sort of person but to play a primary role in choosing the sort of person we will eventually become.

Is it possible that our demand for harsh sentencing guidelines and severe prison conditions are due in part to the sorts of movies and television programs we choose to watch? It's an interesting question, especially now that the Wisconsin state general fund allocates more money to corrections than to higher education. Are we more likely to see our fellow citizens as threats to be punished than as neighbors to be helped? Are we prepared to pay the costs of our entertainments?

June 6, 2010

15. INDUSTRIOUSNESS

Charles Murray's recent book, *Coming Apart: The State of White America,* documents the growing separation between professional and working classes over the past 50 years.

But he doesn't look just at the income gap; instead he examines cultural differences through the lens of four "virtues" that shaped American identity during the eighteenth century: industriousness, honesty, marriage, and religiosity. Of those four virtues, industriousness is key. "If just one American virtue may be said to be defining," Murray observes, "industriousness is probably it."

In 1960, 81% of working class households in Murray's study group had someone working at least 40 hours per week, but by 2008 the number had fallen to 60%. During that time period the percentages for professional class households hasn't changed significantly.

An even more revealing statistic is that the percentage of working class men, age 30–49, who reported themselves as "out of the labor force" in 1963 was 3%; in 2008 the figure had quadrupled to 12%. This is despite advances in health care and improved workplace accommodations for disabilities which should have increased the percentage Americans able to work.

Murray attributes the change not to economic conditions but to a shift in attitude. Americans as a whole, he says, but especially working class white males, don't value hard work as much as they did 50 years ago. In other words, the working class is getting lazier.

In the end I find Murray's analysis of his statistics less than convincing, because he doesn't measure ways in which a change in attitudes may manifest differently among the different classes. Could it be that members of the professional class are spending more time at work but actually working less? Consider, for example, that fantasy football is estimated to have cost American companies $9 billion in lost work time during the past football season and that the average participant earns $80,000 per year.

But even if Murray's answers aren't entirely convincing, the questions he raises are fascinating.

In his autobiography, Benjamin Franklin included "industry" among his key virtues. (You might recall that Franklin is the author of popular sayings like "Early to bed, early to rise, makes a man healthy, wealthy, and wise.") Whereas Murray measures industriousness by employment statistics, Franklin thought of it more broadly. He characterized it this way: "lose no time; be always employed in something useful; cut off all unnecessary actions."

Franklin was a businessman, a politician, and a scholar, and the virtue of industry applied to all three areas of his life. In the eighteenth century, politics and education were considered leisure activities, something one did when one was not working. But they required effort and attention, so industry applied to them as well.

The opposite of industry is considered one of the seven deadly sins. Sloth, or what the Greeks called "acedia," was not simple laziness but indifference, a lack of concern. Industry, by contrast, comes from the conviction that what one is doing is important, that it is worthy of one's full attention.

It seems to me that what has happened during my lifetime reflects a corruption both of the idea of work and of leisure. When work is reduced to money-making and leisure to entertainment, the notion of both of them contributing something essential to the common good is lost.

Is it a coincidence that since 1960, when Murray's study begins, 42 states have created lotteries to help fund education?

Lotteries, in fact, have done nothing to improve education, but they do encourage reliance upon luck, the very opposite of the virtue of industriousness.

In the Midwest we take pride in our work ethic. We tell our children that hard work and delayed gratification are the foundations of success; at the same time we fund their education with a lottery, a practice that rewards blind chance and the thrill of getting something for nothing. What's wrong with this picture?

A society that doesn't pay attention to what it is doing, or thinks what it is doing doesn't matter, especially when it comes to educating its children, is a society that doesn't care. That, by the way, is the definition of sloth, and it isn't confined to the working class.

March 11, 2012

16. Leisure

"Sometimes I just feel like giving up." This from a person I've always admired for her energy and enthusiasm, her passion for worthy causes, and her ability to encourage others to achieve more than they thought possible.

Yet I knew just how she felt: tired, unappreciated, and wondering whether the extra effort she put forth really made any difference. She was experiencing "burnout," which afflicts nearly everyone from time to time.

Burnout is generally thought to come from working too much. The suggested remedy is to spend less time working, in order to balance the work-life scale.

Yet the phrase "work-life balance" is a misnomer. It is not as if we have "work" on one side of the scale and "life" on the other side. What one needs, instead, is "balance in life," a steady diet of activity that is meaningful and life-giving to balance the necessary but tedious activities that are repetitive, dull, and energy draining.

In other words, the person who is experiencing burnout is generally not suffering from too much work, but from the wrong kind of work, or the wrong kinds of leisure activities, which don't give her enough energy to get through the more tedious tasks that comprise the bulk of each day.

What kinds of activities give a person energy? The particulars differ considerably from one person to another, but there are some general characteristics: (1) Meaningful—contributing to something worthwhile; (2) Creative—making or transforming into something new and valuable; (3) Relational—deepening one's relationships with others.

Many activities done during one's time off are actually energy draining rather than restorative. Watching TV, for example, may be fun, but one feels less energized at the end of it, not more. And the average American spends close to three hours per day watching TV.

Burnout is not a recent phenomenon. It is as old as humanity. It is what Thoreau was referring to when he said that "the mass of men lead lives of quiet desperation." It is what Thomas Acquinas called "acedia," a listlessness of the spirit.

The Hebrews introduced the Sabbath as an antidote to burnout. The seventh day was not simply a break from work, but a time for renewal, a place from which to gain perspective, to pray, and study, and reflect on the meaning of life in community with others.

The ancient Greeks spoke of *schola,* generally translated as "leisure," from which we get the term "school." Whereas we tend to think the purpose of schools (and universities) is preparing young people for work, the Greeks thought of work as what one did in order to be able to go to school—that is, in order to have leisure.

Work is what one must do in order to survive; leisure is what one chooses to do. And it is through one's choices that identity is formed.

Americans put a great deal of energy into improving the workplace. There are seminars on employee engagement, policies to prevent bullying and harassment, programs to encourage fitness, specialists in workplace ergonomics.

But for all our attention to workplace improvement, we do a lousy job of managing our leisure time. And that's partly due to language. We tend to associate not working with doing nothing. Hence expressions like "weekend," "vacation," "time off," "retirement," all of which imply emptiness or negation.

Why does the phrase "retirement planning" refer only to finances? Is it because we don't think about preparing ourselves to engage meaningfully and productively in the life of the community once we have finished work?

   If one's time away from work is not used wisely, then the weekend becomes just another part of a series of "one damn thing after another" that actually contributes to burnout instead of preventing it. As Sr. Laurien Pieterek was fond of saying, "we are human beings, not human doings." If we try to define ourselves merely by the work we do, sooner or later we lose sight of the point of it all.

July 17, 2011

17. INVESTMENT

A recent nationwide survey found that only 45% of Americans are satisfied with their jobs. The percentage is down from 52% in 2005 and 61% in 1987. (See the report from The Conference Board, "U.S. Job Satisfaction at Lowest Level in Two Decades," January 5, 2010, www.conference-board.org.)

In 2008 the Gallup organization conducted a similar poll and reported that 90% of American workers said that they were either "completely satisfied" or "partially satisfied" with their jobs. Only 9% reported being somewhat or completely dissatisfied. That nearly matched the highest result for the decade. (See "U.S. Workers' Job Satisfaction Relatively High," July 21, 2008 www.gallup.com).

It is hard to know what conclusions to draw from surveys like this, not only because the findings of the two surveys appear to contradict one another, but because we don't get to see the raw data. What we typically get are news stories based upon press releases from the organizations sponsoring the studies. And without knowing what questions were asked, by whom, in what context, etc., we can't discover the reasons for the discrepancy.

But there are other reasons why it is difficult to draw reliable conclusions from such studies. For one thing, there are so many factors to be taken into consideration. Do people feel less satisfied at work because they are working harder, or because they feel that their work is less meaningful? Do people expect more from the workplace than they did in the past? Is dissatisfaction in the workplace due to increased stress in households? Is the feeling of satisfaction in the workplace tied to confidence in the economy? There are dozens of questions such as these we would need to know the answer to before we would be justified in drawing any practical conclusions. (By "practical conclusion" I mean some action that the leader of an organization might take in order to address the "problem" of dissatisfaction at his or her workplace.)

Aristotle said that you "can't demand more precision than the subject matter allows." And satisfaction is one of those subjects that doesn't allow much precision. In Aristotle's time the Greek word for satisfaction was *eudaimonia,* which meant, literally, having a "good spirit;" it is usually translated as "happiness."

The problem is, we don't know much about what makes us happy, and therefore we aren't very good at answering questions about how happy we are (or what would make us more happy, or less unhappy).

According to Tom Rath, a researcher at the Gallup organization, people who have a "best friend" at work are seven times more likely to express high levels of job satisfaction. Yet, "friendship" rarely even rates among the things that workers seek when choosing employment. When seeking a new job people tend to look for the sorts of things they want, such as type of work, pay level, benefits, vacation time, location, opportunities for advancement, and so forth. But those things are not nearly as highly correlated with happiness as the quality of one's social relationships.

Not only do people not think about friendship as a key factor in their own satisfaction at work, they tend to discount its value in their personal lives. Daniel Gilbert, a Harvard psychology professor who wrote *Stumbling on Happiness,* says that "social relationships are the single most important ingredient of happiness," and yet when he asked people what they would do if they had to choose between losing their best friend and losing their eyesight, they overwhelmingly said they would prefer to lose their best friend. This is despite the fact that people who are blind tend to be just as happy as people with sight, but people who do not have friends are miserable.

The Conference Board report on job satisfaction was covered by nearly every major news outlet in the United States. The widespread interest in its findings seems to be due to the fact that we are anxious about where our country is heading. Are we going up or down, and how fast, and how far?

But I think the significance of the report does not lie in the evidence it purports to provide about the quality of life in America today. Instead, its chief significance lies in the encouragement it gives each one of us to ask, once again, what really makes me happy? Am I looking for the right things? Have I been putting enough into my friendship account?

January 17, 2010

EDUCATION

18. History

We live in an ahistorical society.

It's not just that we don't know much history, it's that we think it is largely irrelevant, so we don't pay attention to it.

This is due to the myth of progress, which can be traced back in literature to the nineteenth century, with writers such as Herbert Spencer, Charles Darwin, and H. G. Wells. But the myth also has roots in the popular effects of the scientific age, in the practical effects of scientific application upon society, which inclines us to think that the next new thing is inevitably an improvement upon the last old thing. For the most part this is a subconscious attitude, and it is expressed in a multitude of ways: our tendency to value youth and disparage age; our attentiveness to trends and fashions; our brand consciousness; our desire for the new and improved; our preference for the synthetic over the natural; and, most of all, our tendency to read only what has been written in the past few days or months.

The danger of relying too much on present conditions is that we develop a narrow perspective on our own lives and the challenges facing us. We forget that we are not only living in history, we are, to a great extent, products of history. And when we forget this, we begin to think that only our own preferences are valuable.

There are a couple of ways that we can step out of this preoccupation with the present. One is by participating in traditional activities, whether they are civic celebrations such as Oktoberfest, or the ritual of worship, or the activity of politics, sport, music, or dance. G. K. Chesterton referred to tradition as "the democracy of the dead." It is a way of keeping the past alive to us in our daily activities, of allowing those who have gone before us to have a voice in the way we manage the world.

Another way is to read old books. It is a wise habit to read one book at least a hundred years old for every contemporary book one reads. For every courtroom drama by John Grisham one could read a tragedy by Shakespeare, for every Barbara Kingsolver epic a novel by Jane Austen, for every screed by Marcus Borg a treatise by Athanasius.

Stepping out of our preoccupation with the present will help us to see our contemporary world in a broader context. We will come to see that some ideas that seemed to be new are actually quite old, that some parts of life that seem accidental are actually fundamental to human nature, that some features of our society that seem to demand a quick fix are actually cyclical and will resolve themselves if we are patient enough to ride out the difficulties. In short, we will be better able to distinguish the significant from the urgent, and act upon what we know to be just and good instead of what seems at the time to be necessary.

November 29, 2009

19. Know Yourself

The ancient temple at Delphi had an expression inscribed over the entrance that said "Know Yourself." It seems like an easy task but is, in fact, terribly difficult. Even the most basic questions about ourselves are not easily answered. Am I a product of creation or evolution? Does my personality derive from my genetics or from my environment? Are my moods due to biochemical changes, the people I encounter, or the thoughts I am thinking? Do I control my emotions, or do my emotions control me?

In higher education, we call people who claim to have answers to such questions "experts" in some field or other, such as psychology or biology, or even ethics. (Sometimes, if they think their students are not a sufficient audience, they write newspaper columns so that they will have an even bigger audience to ignore their opinions.) In ancient Greece, the name for such people was "sophists" (literally, "wise ones"), not because they actually were wise but because they claimed to be so.

In what is probably the first and, I think, still the best text ever written on ethics, Plato's *Apology,* Socrates calls himself a philosopher (from *philo* or "love" and *sophia* or "wisdom") in order to distinguish himself from the sophists. He seemed to believe that the chief cause of human misery in the world was the tendency to think we know what we do not know. So he set himself the task of going about the city, questioning everyone who had a reputation for knowledge, and he discovered that "those who had the highest reputation were nearly the most deficient, while those who were thought to be inferior were more knowledgeable." Exposing the ignorance of those who claimed to be wise created many enemies, and eventually led to his execution.

Because of the widespread tendency toward self-deception, Socrates claimed that the greatest good is not to be virtuous, but to discuss virtue. The sort of discussion he recommended was public questioning of ideas, not information sharing, not propaganda, but a serious give and take of reasons for thinking one way or another. Of course, we live in a society with no shortage of people talking about virtue, but nearly all of the talk is of the condescending sort, people telling but not listening, with little genuine conversation taking place, and only occasional changing of hearts and minds.

Recently I attended a lecture by an individual with impressive credentials. He had many years of professional experience, an Ivy League degree, a list of notable publications, and a confident, self-deprecating manner. His topic was controversial, and he was speaking to an audience that agreed with his conclusions. His reasoning was flawed. The support for his position was all smoke and mirrors and no substance. But nobody questioned him. Instead, they praised the thoroughness of his presentation and the weight of his evidence.

The name for this attitude is *misology*, or dislike of reason. As with many dislikes, it does not announce itself, but instead hides behind a façade of respect. But it is no respect to nod in agreement with nonsense just because it supports a conclusion with which you agree. And it is no disloyalty to question the reasons provided in support of a conclusion with which you agree, if you suspect those reasons to be insufficient.

It is impossible to know ourselves by ourselves. It is even harder to know ourselves among people who encourage our prejudices and want us to encourage their prejudices in return. To know ourselves we must, as Socrates advised, put our ideas out into the public arena, inviting criticism, thanking those who question our reasons, and questioning those who come to our defense.

It is probably wise to beware of those who share our indignations.

April 18, 2010

20. ADVICE

I confess to being a fan of Amy Dickinson's advice column. Yet I wonder how practical advice-giving is. Does the person who needs the advice have the ability to understand and then follow it? Does the person who understands the advice really need it?

In a recent "Ask Amy" column, Baffled Bride wanted to know whether she was justified in scheduling her wedding just two weeks before her cousin's wedding. Her mother was upset because two large weddings so close together would be stressful for the family, but Baffled thought her wedding should be first because she had been engaged for eighteen months and her cousin had been engaged for only eleven months.

What kind of advice could possibly be useful in a situation like this? Ms. Dickinson tells Baffled that she is being "petty and just a little hostile" and that she should change her wedding date. It's good advice, but will it do any good? Will someone who thinks a wedding is a competition be able to understand why she should change the date?

In Jane Austen's *Pride and Prejudice,* Lydia is discovered to have run off with the disreputable Mr. Wickham. Her older sister, Elizabeth, reflecting on the lack of judgment which must have led to such a foolish action, observes that Lydia "has never been taught to think on serious subjects; and for the last half-year...has been given up to nothing but amusement and vanity. She has been allowed to dispose of her time in the most idle and frivolous manner, and to adopt any opinions that came in her way." And it turns out that even after Lydia's reputation has been saved by the timely intervention of her uncle and Mr. Darcy, she is still unable to appreciate her own foolishness. She refuses to listen to any conversation that calls her behavior into question.

Austen's novels are mostly talk. She seems to know that doing what is right requires understanding what is right, and understanding comes through discussion. Her novels bring to mind the famous—and famously controversial—line from Plato's *Apology:* "The greatest good is to discuss virtue every day, for the unexamined life is not worth living for human beings."

Such a claim would not make sense for people who possess a clear and complete understanding of how they should act in the wide variety of circumstances that life presents, but nobody has such comprehensive understanding. The great virtue of Austen's novels is that the most admirable characters are not the ones who think themselves perfect, but the ones who are troubled by their inability to know what to do, and who therefore persist in talking, every day, questioning and being questioned.

Like Jane Austen and Plato, Amy Dickinson seems to understand that there is no set of rules that will provide infallible guidance on how to live—no foolproof rules, that is, for how to run a company, how to raise children, or how to be a friend. Rules are only as reliable as the judgment of the person who comprehends them. Good judgment isn't acquired in a few hours or a few days. You can't go to the library and check out a copy of *Good Judgment for Idiots.* But you can talk about how to live. You can keep trying to figure things out, a little bit at a time.

Maybe advice isn't very useful for the person who needs it most. But a good advice column may be useful to the reader for whom it constitutes a small part of her daily conversation about how to live well. If you don't agree, just go ask Amy.

June 27, 2010

21. FAIRY TALES

One of the chief things my siblings and I are grateful for is a mother who read to us every evening when we were very young.

The list of remembered bedtime stories is long—*Winnie-the-Pooh, Mother Goose, Richard Scarry's Busy Busy World, Uncle Remus*—but my favorites were the fairy tales compiled by the Brothers Grimm. In those days Walt Disney was busy sanitizing the classic stories, removing the parts regarded as too violent and gruesome for impressionable young minds. Fortunately for us, we had an old battered edition which still retained the offending passages, and so we listened with terror and delight as Hansel and Gretel were taken prisoner by the witch, Jack snuffed out the giant, and Red Riding Hood's grandmother was swallowed by the wolf.

It wasn't until many years later that I read Bruno Bettelheim's brilliant defense of fairy tales, *The Uses of Enchantment*, and came to understand why those stories are so significant. According to Bettelheim, every child perceives the world as full of confusion and dangers. All adults are giants. Parents give and withhold affection for reasons that are mysterious and arbitrary. Calamities occur without reason or explanation.

As Bettelheim says, "Although we like to think of young children's lives as free of troubles, they are in fact filled with disappointment and frustration. Children wish for so much, but can arrange so little of their own lives, which are so often dominated by adults without sympathy for the children's priorities. That is why children have a much greater need for daydreams than adults do. And because their lives have been relatively limited they have a greater need for material from which to form daydreams."

Fairy tales acknowledge the child's perception and also give them the assurance to find their way in the world successfully. The heroes of fairy tales use their wits, make wise choices, earn the friendship of allies, and escape from seemingly impossible predicaments.

Stories not only provide children with experiences they normally wouldn't have, some stories, and fairy tales in particular, simplify things to their basic components—good and bad actors, failures and successes, curses and blessings. They allow the child to reflect upon the ways behaviors shape a life for good or ill.

The best stories successfully engage the child's imagination by allowing the child to feel what it is like to be in danger, to be rescued, to rescue another, to offer and receive hospitality, to seek and grant forgiveness. They enlarge the range of experiences a child may have, and allow the child to have those experiences repeatedly by reading the stories over and over.

Aristotle believed that character traits are formed initially by our basic perception of the world. That is why a child's upbringing is all important. If children are not brought up to perceive things correctly, and to have correspondingly appropriate emotional responses to situations, then it will be difficult for them to think clearly about ethics when they reach adulthood. They won't be able to understand the words or actions of good people.

A child who has not been brought up to experience generosity will not be able to appreciate the ways in which being generous enhances one's relationships with others. She will tend to assume that generous people are foolish. She will think that the best thing to do is always acquire more and more for herself.

A child who has not been brought up to experience justice will lack a sense of proportion, of what is due to oneself and others, and as an adult will tend to become outraged by minor events and complacent in the face of things that really matter.

A child who has not been brought up with a sense of reverence will tend as an adult to think that all talk of faith is a matter of either superstition or indoctrination. He will be impatient with any discussion of the divine, not having any way of judging for himself the difference between the prosaic and the profound.

There is a great deal more to moral development than just reading stories, but the right stories provide an important basis for all further progress. And that's a gift all parents can give their children.

May 6, 2012

22. Freedom and Belonging

On the afternoon of September 24th, a rowdy, drunken mob formed along Vine Street, trashing the street and lawns, damaging cars, creating havoc in a community that prides itself on neighborliness and a spirit of good will. Many of the participants were university students.

It was not an isolated incident. Similar riots, involving drunken students, overturned cars, and destruction of property have happened throughout the U.S. recently in university neighborhoods in Minnesota, Ohio, Oregon, New York, and Michigan.

I teach at a university. And like many educators, I take satisfaction in believing that I am doing my part to help young people mature, to discover their talents, and to use those talents to make the world a better place.

But when events like these happen, I begin to question whether I'm part of the problem. Are we teaching the wrong things, or teaching in the wrong ways, or are there larger cultural factors at work? Perhaps it is all of the above.

Most students go to a university to find their place in the world. They go seeking the knowledge, skills, and experience that will help them get a job, settle into a community, perhaps buy a house and start a family. They desire belonging.

Yet they also desire freedom. They seek the knowledge, skills, and experience that will enable them to have more choices, to travel, to find opportunities, not to be bound by the necessities of preexisting ties.

This dual desire—for freedom and belonging—will persist throughout their lives. Whether they find happiness depends to a large extent on how well they manage to harmonize these two competing desires. Belonging without freedom becomes oppressive; freedom without belonging becomes destructive.

Universities excel at satisfying the desire for freedom. We even have an expression for the kind of freedom that comes from education: "upward mobility." But it could instead be called "outward mobility," because moving up often requires moving out and away—to another company, another city, even another country.

Nearly all of our nation's educational system is designed to teach the priority of freedom over belonging. The standardized tests by which K–12 performance is judged consist of general knowledge and skills, not familiarity with the particular. The U.S. Department of Education isn't interested in whether students know the names of their neighbors across the street or the plants, fish, and birds of the Upper Mississippi River. And professional associations, which have increasing influence over the curriculum in universities, are interested only in national standards, not local engagement.

Of course, general skills and national standards are important, but they need to be balanced by ties to the local and the particular. Otherwise there is no context for meaningful ethical development.

Ethical obligation is not merely an abstract, rational phenomenon. It is not a matter of simply learning rules for behavior and then following them. Our obligations grow out of our emotional ties.

Numerous research studies show that people do not behave well under conditions of anonymity. (You can see that for yourself. Just view the online version of most newspapers where people can post comments without using their real names.) People tend to act responsibly only within networks of mutual accountability.

In the university setting, networks of mutual accountability are established mainly through the faculty. They are the ones who interact with students on a daily basis. They teach classes, choose the textbooks, advise, counsel, and write letters of recommendation. If they think something is important, it will be passed on to the students.

Do faculty members think local engagement is important? Most of us will say so, but our primary loyalty remains to our respective professions, not our local communities. You can tell by the organizations we belong to.

Until educators figure out how to address the need for belonging, by making meaningful membership in a community an integrated part of university life, we will continue to have misbehavior from overly enthusiastic and misguided undergraduates. In fact, it is surprising it doesn't happen more often. The fact that it doesn't is a credit to the students themselves.

October 9, 2011

23. Boat Building

My first boat was a twelve-foot cedar-strip rowboat made by the Ole Lind Boatworks of Detroit Lakes, Minnesota. Nobody else was interested in a battered old boat with splintered seats and rotted gunwales, but I cared about it and cared for it: painted it in the spring, bailed it out after rainstorms, rowed it all around Wymer Lake, and filled it with fish and memories.

Ole Lind immigrated to the United States in 1902, learned the craft of boat building from Erick Erickson in Alexandria, and then set up his own shop in Detroit Lakes in 1913. He was a true craftsman, in the days when the product of one's hands was a testament to one's character.

After World War II the market for boats changed. People no longer wanted the old hand-crafted wooden boats. They wanted new models made of aluminum or fiberglass. Lind's contemporary, Howard Lund, made the switch, and Lund Boats went on to become the nation's leading manufacturer of aluminum fishing boats. Ole Lind managed to hold out for a couple of decades, but eventually closed up shop.

Something changed when boats went into mass production. Once it became possible to build thousands of boats with identical hulls, manufacturers competed with one another on the basis of ornamentation rather than function. Modern boat building became a matter of adding attractive components to a basic hull, and the final product an assemblage of pre-designed parts rather than a unique piece of craftsmanship.

The same thing has happened with cars, and clothing, and houses. The designers don't build, and the builders don't design.

Has that happened with our lives as well, with the very way we think about how we become who we are?

Since the time of Plato, boat building has served as a metaphor for the art of living. The Stoic philosophers, in particular, believed that just as every stroke of the plane affects the shape of a boat's hull, every decision, every thought, plays a part in shaping who we become.

In this sense, learning how to live is like learning to build a boat. And knowing how to live requires reflection upon the purpose of life, because only when you know what something is for can you distinguish the necessary from the incidental. As Epictetus said, "there is no limit to a thing once it is beyond its measure." In boat building, as with everything in life, design depends on purpose.

Living in a culture of mass production, our greatest challenge may be to help our children define their lives in terms of purpose rather than possessions and to think of their education as a process of shaping life to suit that purpose rather than simply compiling a set of generically useful skills.

But if that's the case, the whole trend of education, from pre-K through college, must change, for the current focus of education is on measuring the acquisition of discrete skills. As if preparing for life was simply a matter of compiling "skill sets," rather than a matter of carefully and deliberately integrating experiences into a unified and purposeful whole.

We all need skills, but perhaps, more importantly, we need to know how to employ those skills in the shaping of our own lives. And, for this, the experience of making things—like boats—is indispensable. Learning a craft is important because it teaches us how to think about our own life as craft, as something that requires judgment, and persistence, and practice, and integration.

Over the years I've found that a person who knows how to make something, how to take raw materials and shape them into objects of usefulness and beauty, always has a measure of wisdom, regardless of his or her level of education.

In these days of widespread cultural dissatisfaction, perhaps we could look to people like Ole Lind and ask what we could learn from them about crafting new, more purposeful, American lives.

September 9, 2012

24. Intelligence

Numerous studies of electronic media usage and multitasking have been conducted over the past few years, and a consensus is beginning to emerge: the more one engages in multitasking, the more distraction becomes a habit. One study even found that "heavy media multitasking" makes one, ironically, less efficient at multitasking. As negative effects become more widely recognized in the workplace, new phrases are introduced, such as "disruption cost," "work fragmentation," "information overload," and "continuous partial attention."

Why is multitasking so popular despite growing evidence of its counter-productivity? Perhaps it is because the technological advances that make multitasking possible (in particular, the portability of electronic media) are designed to answer a deep-seated desire for success, uncritically assumed to consist of achieving more in less time.

Consider the ways we measure educational progress. Standardized tests, IQ tests, the ACT, and the SAT, all measure the ability to recall and manipulate information. The more one can recall, and the faster one can manipulate it, the higher one scores.

We tend to lump the different forms of intelligence together (primarily memory and cleverness) and call it "being smart." We test for smartness; we have societies and honors for smart people; we give scholarships based on evidence of smartness. We reward smart people with jobs that pay well and have a significant effect on the well-being of society. And then, occasionally, we are shocked that somebody "with all that education" should act foolishly or selfishly or irresponsibly. "What are they teaching at business schools (or medical schools, or law schools), anyway?"

The odd thing about our society's fascination with "being smart" is that it has relatively little to do with professional success or success in life generally. Good decision-making is more important, and that requires long-term thinking, foresight, and the ability to sort through the mass of detail and pay attention to what is really significant. In short, good decision-making requires wisdom.

Wisdom was considered by the ancient Greeks to be the most significant of the four cardinal virtues, because it serves as a guide to every other aspect of character. Without wisdom any trait, such as cleverness, courage, creativity, or determination, may be used for destructive purposes. Wisdom is collaborative; it comes from the ability to listen to other people, to really pay attention, to discern the truth, and then put the truth into action. The measure of wisdom is whether one's actions further the common good.

Why do we keep teaching memory and cleverness if what we really want is wisdom? Well, we aren't sure how to teach wisdom, and we certainly don't know how to test for it. There are no multiple choice tests than can quantify a person's wisdom. But we do know how to test recall and manipulation. So we teach that instead.

There is an old joke about a drunken man pacing back and forth under a street lamp looking down at his feet. A passerby stops and asks what he's doing. "I'm looking for my car keys," he says. So the passerby begins pacing under the street lamp as well, looking earnestly for the keys. After about fifteen minutes, he stops, and says: "I don't see your keys anywhere. Are you sure this is where you lost them?" "Oh no," replies the drunk, "I dropped them way over there in front of the bar. But it's no use looking over there; it's so dark you can't see a thing."

Our society desperately needs wisdom, but we don't know where to look. And the more we confine our search to the areas illuminated by the multiple input streams of modern tech-nology, the less likely we are to find it.

January 30, 2011

25. TEACHING ETHICS

For over two-thousand years, western societies have been operating under the assumption that education makes citizens more civilized, which is to say, less violent, more respectful toward one another, more ethical.

The Roman poet Ovid expressed a common sentiment when he wrote that, "a faithful study of the liberal arts humanizes character and permits it not to be cruel."

Yet Rome's cruelty was unmatched in the ancient world.

In the 1930s Germany was arguably the world's most civilized nation. It used its sophisticated educational system to perpetrate mass murder. Many of the Nazi officers were highly educated. Adolf Eichmann, in charge of transporting Jews to extermination camps, even cited Immanuel Kant's ethical theory at his trial.

All of this raises the question: Why has two-thousand years of experience with education not resulted in societies that are more ethical, more tolerant, and less prone to violence? Is it even possible to teach ethics?

Controversy over this question can be traced back to the earliest writings on ethics. Aristotle thought virtue results from socialization. Good character traits are taught first at home and then in society. As good behaviors are repeated they become habitual, and the habits gradually become virtues. On this view the chief goal of education is to take amoral children and "form" them into good citizens.

When Tennyson wrote that nature is "red in tooth and claw," he was taking sides with Aristotle, as was Hobbes, who famously observed that life in the state of nature is "solitary, poor, nasty, brutish, and short." Civilization is needed to restrain natural impulses.

Most people tend to agree with Aristotle. The word "education" has almost come to be synonymous with "training," just as the word "ethics" in some circles has become synonymous with "compliance."

A contrasting view originates with Plato. He believed that human beings are innately good. The goal of education is not to form good character traits but rather to reconnect people with their sense of right and wrong. We do this not through training but by listening carefully to one another's words.

Recent studies on empathy support the innate goodness side of the debate. Human beings seem to be neurologically "wired" for friendship, sharing, and compassion, but as we grow up we are "rewired" by cultures of competition, greed, and violence.

How does this happen?

For 30 years, Carol Gilligan has been listening to the voices of young girls and boys, paying attention to how they speak about identity and relationships. Her first book, *In a Different Voice*, pointed out the significance of the distinct ways girls and boys tend to talk about moral problems.

According to Gilligan, what passes for normal development is largely a process of dissociation—detachment from self and other—that takes place at around age 5–6 for boys and age 12–13 for girls. In the case of boys, this can be heard in the adoption of a masculine voice, the bravura that armors them on the playground and protects them from one another's ridicule. In the case of girls, it can be heard in a lessening of confidence and curiosity, a loss of voice that keeps them from asserting themselves in the "wrong" ways.

Such dissociation is not inevitable, but it is common, and it results in young people with a damaged sense of moral integrity, a sense that they are not a single, unified person, not quite whole. Many people never recover the voice that they lost as a child, but they recognize it when they encounter it, especially in characters like Scout in *To Kill a Mockingbird*.

In order to retain that voice of integrity, children need strong, encouraging, and loving relationships. Such relationships are also the key for adults who need their humanity restored.

It may sound trite, but the moral of Gilligan's story is that goodness does not come from education. It comes from good people.

When good people are involved in parenting and educating—when they don't forget that their loving presence is more important than whatever strategy, or system, or outcomes they are employing—they will have a good influence.

Education is essential to society, but it does not necessarily make people more ethical. Listening with a loving presence is what builds trust. And trust makes people—whether individuals or communities—whole.

March 24, 2013

26. Evaluation

In the movie *Crimes and Misdemeanors,* Clifford Stern (played by Woody Allen) says to his niece, "Don't listen to what your teachers tell you. Don't pay attention. Just see what they look like, and that's how you'll know what life's really gonna be like."

It's a throwaway line in the movie, but it rings true to me: first, because it echoes an idea repeated throughout centuries of great literature about teaching, namely, that students choose to learn from people they respect and admire; second, because it confirms my own experience, that the teachers from whom I learned the most where those who loved life, and they expressed that love by profound interest in their students' well-being and in their passion for whatever they happened to be teaching.

Mr. Hovde managed to get an entire class of 17 year olds to do algebraic proofs, day after day, for an entire year. We didn't know why it was important, and he never managed to explain it to our satisfaction, but he loved math, and he thought that doing proofs was the purest expression of mathematical reasoning, so he assigned them, and we did them, and got good at doing them, because we liked him and wanted to earn his respect.

This week the Wisconsin Department of Public Instruction rolled out the "School Report Card" which gives every public school in the state an "accountability index score" to indicate how they measure up in preparing students to meet newly developed academic standards.

This is part of a national push by the U.S. Department of Education to rescind the unpopular No Child Left Behind initiative and replace it with programs designed by each state to link school and teacher performance to internationally benchmarked standards.

The national trend in educational reform is great for the burgeoning school testing industry, but is it good for students?

Deborah Kenny, founder of Harlem Village Academies (a New York charter school network), does not think so.

In a recent editorial in the *New York Times,* she argued that "Some of the new government proposals for evaluating teachers, with their checklists, rankings and ratings, have been described as businesslike, but that is just not true. Successful companies do not publicly rate thousands of employees from a central office database; they don't use systems to take the place of human judgment. They trust their managers to nurture and build great teams, then hold the managers accountable for results."

A more efficient statewide system of evaluation will not necessarily make poor teachers better, but it may keep good teachers from doing what they do best—sharing their passion for the subjects they teach in ways that may be idiosyncratic but which nevertheless manage to connect with students in a particular time and context.

How can measuring teaching effectiveness make teaching worse? By overlooking the fact that good teaching consists of an initiation into the intellectual virtues, such as curiosity, perseverance, and discernment. These virtues are difficult to measure because, like all virtues, they take a long time to come to fruition (and educational measurements are necessarily short-term), and they can only be evaluated by closely observing the person who embodies them.

This means that they don't get measured, and the more efficient a school system is at teaching the measurables, the less time will be spent on the significant, but non-measureable qualities like the intellectual virtues that form the basis for lasting success.

When I look back at the teachers who most influenced my

own education, I realize that they really did show us what life would look like. Because Mr. Hovde cared about us, he talked to us about his loves: hitting the road on his Harley Davidson, coaching wrestling, and hanging out with Ms. Nelson (the school librarian). But he also showed us, by his passion for mathematical proofs, that with sufficient time and attention, any problem can be solved, and that the difference between right and wrong is not a matter of opinion, but discernment.

Mr. Hovde would not have fared well under the new teacher evaluation system. His class changed my life, yet my test scores would have revealed gaps in preparation for college-level math. And that makes me wonder, will our best teachers have any place in the brave new world of educational reform?

October 21, 2012

27. COMMENCEMENT

On Monday President Barack Obama gave a commencement address to the graduates of Booker T. Washington High School in Memphis, Tennessee. I happened to be in Memphis that day, having arrived over the weekend for an unrelated event.

I had expected to hear people talking mostly about the flooding Mississippi River, but that wasn't the case. The river was still very high, but it was old news. Instead, folks were talking about the surprising run of the Memphis Grizzlies in the NBA playoffs and President Obama's visit.

Even though the President generated a great deal of talk, there seemed to be comparatively little interest in what he was going to say. But after all, it was a commencement address. What is there to say?

Few graduation speeches are memorable. Of the dozens I have endured, one in particular stands out because the speaker managed to put nearly everyone in the audience to sleep. Of course, putting people to sleep is not that difficult (I've done it myself), but to accomplish it during a celebratory occasion when people are sitting in uncomfortable chairs—that takes talent.

Graduation speeches are generally unremarkable because the themes are so predictable. First, there are three versions of the time speech: "Cherish Your Memories;" "Live in the Present;" and "You are the Future." Another common theme is encouragement, as in the "Make a Difference" speech or the "Don't Give Up" speech. A third theme is introspection, in which graduates are urged to "Be True to Yourself" or to go out and "Discover Yourself." Finally, there is "The Importance of Education" speech. This tends to be the worst. It is the speech most likely to put people to sleep. The time to talk about why kids should go to school isn't the day they are finally getting out of school. Unless, of course, you are the president, in which case people will keep themselves awake by cheering or booing regardless of what you say.

That's pretty much it. The difference between a good graduation speech and a poor graduation speech resides not in theme but in execution. As the architect Mies van der Rohe famously said: "God is in the details."

President Obama gave an "encouragement/importance of education" speech. That's a challenging combination, but he got the details right.

Obama acknowledged the importance of a change in attitude for the amazing turnaround that Booker T. Washington High School has had in recent years. "You didn't just create a new curriculum, you created a new culture—a culture that prizes hard work and discipline; a culture that shows every student here that they matter and that their teachers believe in them." He praised the students, the parents, and the teachers for working together to be successful. "You inspire me," he said.

Education is important, he continued, because it is transformative: the qualities developed through sustained hard work "change how we see ourselves." When education is done right, students acquire "empathy, discipline, the capacity to solve problems, and the capacity to think critically." Such qualities are necessary because they prepare young people for public life and thus make our country better.

In emphasizing the transformative role of education, Obama expressed a classical view of schools as places where students learn how to become citizens. To commence is to "begin." Commencement marks the passage into the public life of the community. It's an important occasion, worthy of a presidential address.

I wonder what Lionel Hollins, head coach of the Memphis Grizzlies, said to get his players to perform so far beyond expectations in the recent playoff series? Probably something like, "This is your time," or "Go out and give it everything you've got!" What else could he say? In the end, the words don't matter that much. It's just important that the coach say something. He has to show that he believes in the team.

That's what President Obama did Monday for the graduates of Booker T. Washington. And that's what speakers across the region will be doing for our graduates in the coming days.

May 22, 2011

CIVILITY

28. Conversation

When politicians and pundits call for more civility in public life, what, precisely, are they calling for? Do they simply want people to be nicer to one another, or do they want something more substantial?

After all, being nice is not the same as being good. And even though we stress to children the importance of being nice, it is but the first step toward mature ethical behavior, not the final one.

Preschool teachers know that one of the first things children need to learn is how to use words to settle disputes. At first, they need to learn what words to use; later, once they've learned the words, they need to be reminded to use them. It's not unusual to hear a teacher on the playground, in an effort to turn aside a confrontation, say something like: "Emma, use your words."

Adults also need reminding, not only about what words to use, but how and when to use them. That's because words are the principal means by which we give shape and meaning to our lives. To refuse to speak to another, or to use words only to bully, disparage, coerce, or manipulate, is to treat others as less than human, as not worthy of full participation in the human community.

The word "conversation" still carries in its origins the remnants of this rich meaning. It comes from two Latin words, *con* ("together") and *vertere* ("to turn"), and it suggests that the ways in which we speak to one another are what bring us together. But it also implies that words may be used to drive us apart. It is significant that the Latin word for sin was *aversio,* literally, "to turn away."

For most of its history, the word "conversation" referred

to something like "a way of life." It would be used to describe someone whose words and actions expressed peace and integrity, an attitude of getting along with others. Paintings by Dutch artists Vermeer and Ter Borch were called "conversation pieces," not because they provided something to talk about, but because they depicted a way of live characterized by domestic tranquility.

The King James Version of the Bible, from 1611, translated Philippians 3:20 as "For our conversation is in heaven," suggesting that heaven is the place where people turn together in peace. There is no other word in the English language that so succinctly expresses the notion that our daily words and actions constitute the very quality of our lives together.

"Civility" is the contemporary word we commonly use to express our desire for peaceful discourse. But it is a poor substitute for "conversation": it suggests a superficial politeness, for one can keep a civil tongue while harboring deep resentments.

Discourse that seems uncivil may in fact be constructive. Healthy disagreements are the very lifeblood of a family, or an organization, or a community. Disagreements can reveal passionate commitments to an idea or a cause.

Apathetic civility is not a desirable condition, but healthy disagreement is. In healthy disagreement people take turns pointing out errors of thought in order that both sides may reach a shared understanding.

Though both divisive speech and argumentative speech may look the same on the surface, they are driven by entirely different motivations. While divisive speech uses words to coerce, manipulate, or deceive in order to gain some particular outcome, argumentative speech uses criticism in order to correct error or enhance understanding, to get people to a state of agreement.

What is so discouraging about much of our current public discourse is that words are routinely used in ways that undermine community by turning people against one another, but they are rarely used to engage others in serious dialogue about substantive issues. In short, we have too much divisive speech and not enough argumentative speech.

Being civil to one another is important, but it alone does not determine the quality of public discourse. As the character Frank Burns says in an episode of M*A*S*H, "It's nice to be nice—to the nice." He could have added that it's better to be good—to everyone.

June 17, 2012

Every fall, as Oktoberfest season comes around, I hear apologies being made for the city of La Crosse, as in: "La Crosse is a great place to live, but…it's not very diverse."

It is a commonplace in American society that we should celebrate diversity. But why is diversity important? And how is it best celebrated?

In one sense, La Crosse is not very diverse: its inhabitants are overwhelming white, Lutheran or Catholic, German or Norwegian.

In another sense, however, the very fact that La Crosse has an identifiable cultural heritage and that the community comes together annually to celebrate that heritage is what makes it distinct from many other American cities.

Imagine for a moment that every community in the world was equally diverse, that every town, city, and state had a proportionate representation of the world's cultural, social, political, racial, religious, gender, and age groups. Would that be a better world than the one we inhabit now?

It would undoubtedly be more equal, but I cannot help thinking it would be less interesting and less fulfilling—and even, ironically, less diverse. Without communities of shared characteristics there is no culture, and without culture, there is no diversity.

The idea of diversity has meaning only against a backdrop of groups of people joined together by their shared characteristics. In other words, the value of diversity requires a context of commonality.

One of the old Bugs Bunny cartoons features a king who complains to his chef, "Every day it's the same old thing—variety!" What he wants instead is plain old rabbit stew, so he demands, "I want some hasenpfeffer!" Variety may be the spice of life, but you can't live on spices.

The biggest problem with the term "diversity" is that it doesn't help us make crucial distinctions about the kinds of differences we should appreciate and those we should not. It does not help us to form an opinion about cultural practices such as polygamy, arranged marriage, witchcraft, vengeance killings, female circumcision, and so on. To form opinions about such controversial practices we must rely upon more robust notions, such as respect, dignity, freedom, and natural human rights.

Using the term "diversity" to set a social agenda is misleading. It suggests that everything is valuable—every person, every trait, every custom, every practice. But that's not the case. What we really value in other people is not difference, but goodness.

However, goodness is expressed in so many different ways that we need to keep an open mind in order to recognize it.

Instead of diversity, we should encourage hospitality— the ancient virtue of welcoming the stranger. Sharing a meal, talking together, finding out how we differ as well as what we have in common—that is the only way to really earn mutual respect. In the sharing of hospitality, we participate in difference, but we discover goodness.

As globalization becomes the new normal, and people acquire more freedom to travel, to interact with people from other cultures, and to experiment with different lifestyles, the real champions of diversity are not those who "appreciate difference," but those who commit themselves to continuing the particular practices and traditions that bind communities together: the old man who plays jazz trumpet every Wednesday night on Beale Street; the Canadian grandmother who teaches her grandchildren how to make chokecherry jelly; the Mongolian youths who spend years perfecting the skill of riding horses.

La Crosse should be proud of its heritage. Personally, I

could be perfectly content without ever hearing "Beer Barrel Polka" again in my lifetime. But I'm glad there are people who enjoy it and places like La Crosse where people are passionate enough about their community to dress up in leather breeches, drink beer from a golden keg, eat hasenpfeffer, and dance the polka until they get blisters on their bunions.

It may not be for everyone. But you have to admit—it's different.

September 11, 2011

30. Minor Differences

Growing up, our favorite winter playground game was "King of the Mountain," played on a huge snow pile behind the school. We would divide into teams: Arctic Cat and Ski-Doo. The battles were fiercely fought: noses were bloodied, teeth were lost, and if there were no broken bones, it was only because the robust winter parkas cushioned every fall.

To those engaged in the battle, the gulf between one side and the other was immeasurable. It seemed obvious to those of us on the Arctic Cat team that our snowmobiles were faster, more powerful, more durable, could go through deeper snow, could jump higher, looked better, and had better names. To the Ski-Doo team, the comparisons seemed equally obvious and one-sided, though favoring the yellow over the black.

It never occurred to us that there were kids in states like Florida who had never heard of either Arctic Cat or Ski-Doo, and if they had, would have thought them virtually identical.

Sigmund Freud observed that "it is precisely the minor differences in people who are otherwise alike that form the basis of feelings of strangeness and hostility between them" ("The Taboo of Virginity," 1918). He used the expression "narcissism of minor differences" to describe the way in which people exaggerate slight differences between themselves and others as a way of establishing their self-identity. The less substantial the differences actually are, the more one feels the need to aggressively defend them.

What this means is that groups are defined not so much by the actual differences that divide them, but by the willingness to defend the importance of those differences. The less substantial the difference, the more anger is required to disguise the lack of substance.

There is an old Star Trek episode titled "Let That Be Your Last Battlefield" in which everyone on the planet Ariannus has a face that is half black and half white. The planet is engaged in a civil war: those with black on the right side of their faces against those with black on the left side of their faces. The crew of the Enterprise cannot understand why they are fighting. To Lokai, the leader of the rebels, it is as clear as the nose on his face.

When Michael Ignatieff was a journalist covering the war in Croatia in the early 1990s, he wanted to understand why the Serbs and Croats were killing one another. After all, to most Americans, the two cultures were virtually identical, and they had been living peaceably together as neighbors in the same cities and villages for many years. He asked a Serbian soldier to explain the difference between them, since he himself couldn't tell them apart. "See this? These are Serbian cigarettes," the soldier said. "Over there, they smoke Croatian cigarettes."

It seems to be an intrinsic part of human nature to choose sides first and create reasons for our choice afterwards. Perhaps this is how we create an identity for ourselves, how we define who we are and what our purpose is. But it has the unfortunate consequence that our discussions of ethical issues are rarely genuine. They are nearly always constrained by the political culture.

If you don't believe me, try having a discussion about abortion, or homosexuality, or drug use, in which you ask genuine questions about the effects of those practices on individuals and communities, and where you insist on acknowledging both the positives and negatives of each wherever you find them. What if someone found evidence that children raised by lesbian couples developed a greater than average sense of well-being and maturity, but that those raised by gay couples was lower than average?

Civility

In these politically contentious times, it is hard to have a reasonable discussion about ethical issues without it turning into a partisan power struggle. As a Bible-believing, pro-life, gun-toting, tree-hugging, peace-loving, fiscally conservative feminist, I have a hard time knowing what side I'm supposed to be on. Sometimes I feel like the unfortunate kid who tried to start a Polaris team, and got beat up by everybody.

May 16, 2010

31. HOSPITALITY

A few years ago my wife and I were eating lunch at a café when a precocious little girl of about four years old greeted us from a nearby table. As she chatted away happily her mother interrupted: "Mary, didn't I tell you not to talk to strangers?" "Oh," replied the little girl, "they're not strangers; they're nice people!"

It is a sad commentary on our society that so many parents emphasize the harm strangers may cause but neglect to teach their children the blessings of the chance encounter, a lesson that is at the heart of hospitality.

In many countries around the world, the virtue of love (or charity) is demonstrated through acts of hospitality. Early Christians valued hospitality both because it expressed the love of others as beings created in the image of God and because it furthered development of all the other virtues. Hospitality, in short, was regarded as the form of the virtues: each of the virtues comes to fruition in the practice of hospitality.

Hospitality is traditionally understood as taking care of the needs of strangers, which in most cultures requires inviting the stranger into one's home. In the United States today, we speak of the "hospitality industry"—principally hotels and restaurants—which, ironically, allow the needs of strangers to be met without actually entering into anyone's home. A traveller may visit the local attractions, have dinner, and stay the night, exchanging no more than a handful of words with residents of the city.

In wealthy societies, the needs of the stranger—the traveller, the homeless, the sick, the mentally ill, the disabled, and the elderly—are provided mainly by institutions. Wherever there are needs, there are professionals dedicated to meeting those needs. But this institutionalization of care, which is intended to make sure no one's needs are left unmet, comes at a cost that is more than financial. It greatly diminishes the opportunities for hospitality among the general population.

Without the regular practice of hospitality, which requires outwardly directed actions of loving kindness, people begin to think that love is no more than private emotion. Love changes from gift (something done for the sake of others) to feeling (something one desires). Moreover, as soon as meeting people's needs becomes a commercial transaction, those who cannot pay for their needs become a burden to society, and those who are required to pay taxes to meet the burden begin to feel resentment.

Over the past fifty years or so, as the traditional practice of hospitality has been replaced by publicly funded social services, the promotion of love as a virtue has been abandoned in favor of the less demanding public values of civility and tolerance. Thus, teachers and parents encourage children not to love their neighbors, but instead to "appreciate diversity" and "respect differences." Such contemporary values are not unworthy, but they do no more than set minimal standards for social conduct.

Civility and tolerance express respect for people whose relationships to our own lives are distant and will likely remain so, but hospitality invites strangers into deeper relationship. While civility and tolerance respect other peoples' beliefs, hospitality welcomes actual people into one's life. If we tolerate one another, you can go your way and I can go mine; we simply agree not to harm one another. If we show hospitality to one another, we enter into genuine relationships. And genuine relationships are essential to a flourishing life.

What we really value in others is neither sameness nor difference but complementarity. We are born partial, and only in relationship with others do we discover wholeness. We need to practice hospitality, not because it is a more efficient way to meet the needs of others, but because loving service is itself a need.

If we really love our children, and wish them to have rich, meaningful lives, we should start them out on the right path by encouraging them to talk to strangers.

April 24, 2011

32. OTHER VOICES, OTHER ROOMS

Early in Plato's *Apology,* when Socrates is explaining to the jurors how he came to be disliked by so many people in the city of Athens, he tells the story of his friend, Chairephon, who made a trip to the oracle at Delphi to ask whether any man was wiser than Socrates. The oracle answered, "No one is wiser."

When Socrates heard this, he was suspicious. So he began to question his fellow citizens, especially those who had a reputation for wisdom, and he discovered that the people he questioned generally thought they knew much more than they did. In fact, he noticed that those who thought they knew what they were talking about were more likely to be ignorant than the people who didn't think they knew much.

He said to himself: "I am wiser than this man; it is likely that neither of us knows anything worthwhile, but he thinks he knows something when he does not, whereas when I do not know neither do I think I know; so I am likely to be wiser than he to this small extent, that I do not think I know what I do not know."

This has come to be known as "Socratic wisdom," namely, that wisdom consists in knowing what one does not know.

I had the good fortune to grow up in a small community with a large extended family. Every holiday and birthday, the family would gather together. After a meal, the men would invariably retreat to one room and the women to another. The children were free to do as they pleased, and I remember going from one room to the other listening to the conversations.

The men had two subjects of conversation: hunting and football. Occasionally, someone would bring up politics, but the discussion wouldn't last long. The men already had their minds made up about politics. It was just "common sense," they'd say. Then they would return to hunting and football.

The problem was, there wasn't enough to say about those things to keep the dialogue new and interesting. By the time I was twelve years old I had heard the story of the "Rock Lake Buck" eighty or ninety times. (That was the huge buck that was occasionally glimpsed but nobody ever got a shot at. One year they found his tracks in the snow outside the deer shack in the morning; he had been watching them through the windows while they played cards the night before.) I would hear over and over how Fran Tarkenton could throw the ball and scramble out of trouble, but he just wasn't tough enough; if only he was as tough as Joe Kapp, nobody could beat the Vikings.

The women had endless topics to discuss: church, schools, politics, health care, children, aging, recipes, art, neighbors, television shows, books, music. If somebody brought something up, they talked about it. It didn't matter if they knew anything about the subject. In fact, for them, the reason for talking about something seemed to be to learn more about it.

The men liked to be on solid ground, talking about things all of them were familiar with and could agree on. They talked the way they smoked cigarettes and drank whiskey, to pass the time. The women didn't seem to be interested in passing time, they wanted to use time, to fill it up. An opportunity to talk was an opportunity to learn something, and when I would sit in on their conversations, I would learn something too.

Even to a child it was obvious: the women weren't embarrassed by not knowing something. If they were uncertain, they asked questions and figured it out. The men talked about common sense, but the women employed it.

Most of the essential lessons to be learned from reading the great philosophers can be confirmed in the observation of our daily lives. From Socrates we learn what the women in my childhood already knew, that the first and most important task in becoming wise is not to take a position, but to ask a question.

September 26, 2010

33. The Ethics of Belief

According to a recent survey conducted by the Pew Research Center for the People and the Press, only 59% of Americans believe there is solid evidence of global warming. That is despite near universal agreement among scientists that the earth's temperatures have been increasing steadily for the past several decades. In a situation like this, where the evidence supporting global warming is readily available, easy to understand, and overwhelming, it is morally irresponsible to believe that it is not happening.

We sometimes hear that "everyone is entitled to their own beliefs," as if people can hold any beliefs they want and should never be criticized for them. But that's not really the case. We actually do hold people accountable for their beliefs, especially when those beliefs result in actions that have significant effects on people. If a bicycle thief defends himself in court by saying, "I don't believe in the doctrine of private property," the judge is unlikely to be impressed. Sincerity of belief, in such a case, is not merely irrelevant; it is part of the problem.

What about freedom of speech? Aren't people free to express any beliefs they want to? No, not really. Every society has legal limits upon what kind of speech is acceptable. In the United States people are not legally free to threaten to harm another person, to discuss plans to commit a crime, or to incite people to violence. But beyond restrictions such as this, people generally may say whatever they like, regardless of how foolish it is. People are free to say that global climate change is a conspiracy dreamed up by Al Gore, or that the earth is flat, or that aliens are responsible for crop circles in Iowa. But even though people cannot be legally charged for holding and expressing such ideas, they still can be morally criticized for them, because legal freedom is not the same as moral freedom. In the United States it is legally permissible to publicly deny that the Holocaust took place, but it is morally impermissible to do so. Given the amount of historical evidence, there is no excuse for a reasonably educated person to believe that the Holocaust didn't happen.

Many topics are not so clear-cut, however, and that is why free speech is particularly significant. Most of us are mistaken about many of our beliefs—either they are just flat-out wrong or they are partial, distorted, or biased. The problem is, we don't know which of our beliefs are mistaken, otherwise we would change them. (Like most people, I assume that my beliefs are true and that the people I disagree with hold false beliefs. Of course, the people I disagree with see it differently.) The only way to correct our false beliefs is through conversation—especially by talking with people who know more about something than we do. That is why Socrates famously claimed that "the greatest good is to discuss virtue every day," because acting upon our beliefs is fairly easy, but acquiring true beliefs is hard work.

One of the underappreciated aspects of a democracy is that citizens are—to a certain extent—morally responsible for one another's beliefs. That is not to say everybody is personally responsible for what the people across the street from them believe, but rather that we are all responsible generally for the conversations we have with one another, for participating in public discourse about laws and policies that affect our common life.

Because we are free to participate in political discourse, and we are free to vote on the basis of the opinions formed as a result of that discourse, we are therefore responsible for the content and the character of the discourse in which we participate. Every freedom implies a corresponding duty. If we don't agree with what people are saying, or how they are saying it, we have an obligation to do something about it. And the first and most important thing we should do is talk to them (not about them).

November 21, 2010

34. Divisiveness

Is our society's divisiveness over issues such as abortion, capital punishment, stem cells, health care reform and climate change due to the fact that we have different values, or is it that we tend to see things differently? Or, perhaps, is our tendency to see things differently what we mean by having different values?

In *Life on the Mississippi*, Mark Twain recounts his youth, when he learned to pilot a steamboat on the river. During his first time at the helm, he steers the boat sharply toward shore to avoid what he thinks is a bluff reef and nearly crashes the boat into some tree branches. Mr. Bixby, the pilot, orders him to turn the boat back on course and run over the reef. Twain questions the order, but Bixby is insistent. "I'm taking responsibility," he says. So the young Twain turns the boat toward the reef.

> I...made a straight break for the reef. As it disappeared under our bows I held my breath; but we slid over it like oil.
>
> "Now don't you see the difference? It wasn't anything but a wind reef. The wind does that."
>
> "So I see. But it is exactly like a bluff reef. How am I ever going to tell them apart?"
>
> "I can't tell you. It is an instinct. By and by you will just naturally know one from the other, but you never will be able to explain why or how you know them apart."
>
> It turned out to be true. The face of the water, in time, became a wonderful book—a book that was a dead language to the uneducated passenger, but which told its mind to me without reserve.

Many people believe that ethics consists mainly in having good values. But most people's values don't differ all that much.

Just as every riverboat pilot thinks that you should steer away from dangerous structures, just about every person thinks you should avoid doing things that cause harm to others. Just about everybody in our society believes we should protect innocent lives, provide affordable, quality health care, and have clean air and water.

But just as the most important part of learning to pilot a boat is recognizing what's happening on the river, the most important part of moral education is learning to recognize what's going on in life. If two people can't agree about what's going on, they won't be able to agree on how to act.

We learn about what's going on in the world only partly from direct experience. Most of what we learn is from others, sometimes through conversation, but often mediated by newspaper, television, radio or Internet. That's why our most significant moral obligation to one another as citizens is to speak the truth.

Truth-telling is hard because it requires not only that we want to tell the truth but also that we know what we are talking about, and usually we don't have enough information, or we don't know how much of the information we do have is reliable enough, to be justified in our judgments.

I have known few liars but many people who did not tell the truth. It is easy to resolve not to tell lies; it is difficult to become the sort of person who can tell the truth consistently. It takes patience, experience, and courage, but mostly it requires humility.

When I listen to the diatribes that pass for political discourse on our most divisive issues, I wonder how many "uneducated passengers" we have on our ship of state, ready to praise or blame the crew, but unable themselves to tell a wind reef from a bluff reef.

July 18, 2010

35. Cursing

A couple of weeks ago former Indianapolis Colts head coach Tony Dungy criticized Rex Ryan, head coach of the New York Jets, for frequent cursing during an episode of "Hard Knocks," an HBO series chronicling the Jets' practices. The reaction in the sports world revealed deep differences in attitudes toward the use of foul language. Fellow coaches, players, and sports announcers lined up on different sides of the fence, some agreeing with Dungy, others defending Ryan.

Ryan's defenders said things like this: "It's just words, they don't hurt anybody"; "Ryan is just being himself; if that's how he runs his practices, that's what he should do"; "Dungy should just mind his own business."

Dungy's defenders have been more inclined to soft-pedal their opinions, saying things like: "I agree that Ryan should tone it down, especially when you know that kids will be watching the show"; or "I understand that's what a lot of coaches do, but I personally choose not to do it."

I find it curious that Ryan's defenders are so confident in their response and that Dungy's defenders are so timid. Why do people find it so difficult to express their objections to cursing?

I suspect it's partly because of the strong and commendable tradition in this country of defending free speech. We are reluctant to criticize people's manner of expression, even as we are quick to criticize the content of what they say.

Another reason may be that it's hard to demonstrate the direct harmful effects of cursing. Most of our public moral objections to particular kinds of behavior depend on reasons that show a demonstrable harm.

The majority of people who object to cursing would probably agree that it doesn't amount to a serious harm; rather, it is something that is distasteful or vulgar, like belching in public. A well brought-up person just doesn't do that sort of thing.

But I believe there are more substantial objections, having to do with the role that words play in the public sphere.

Words shape our lives. The laws that constitute our society are made up of words. Oaths and vows, which mark the most significant passages in our lives, are composed of words. Wars are begun with a declaration and ended with a treaty. Long-standing relationships are broken up by an insult and repaired with an apology. Without words we wouldn't have a recognizably "human" life at all.

Iris Murdoch, the British novelist, observed that "we make pictures of ourselves, and then come to resemble the pictures." The chief way we make pictures of ourselves is with words.

Cuss words are, with a few exceptions, words that refer either to sexual anatomy and activity or to excrement. They are typically used to express anger or hatred, or to shock, belittle, ridicule, and demean. The widespread use of cuss words reduces the world to a landscape of sexual objectification and waste, bringing into the public sphere images of things and activities that we normally choose to keep private.

Cuss words present a distorted picture of human beings, a picture that is incompatible with seeing the inherent dignity of every human life. That is why all the major world's religions object to the use of foul language, because it is "blasphemous," an insult to those whom the Creator loves.

Guy Deutscher, a research fellow at the University of Manchester and author of a new book about language and perception, says, "The habits of mind that our culture has instilled in us from infancy shape our orientation to the world and our emotional responses to the objects we encounter." How we talk to people and about people affects how we perceive them; how we perceive them affects how we treat them. And it doesn't matter who is the speaker and who is the hearer; words affect the perception of both.

Dungy's critics accuse him of being a "prude," of being overly sensitive and morally judgmental. Such reactions attempt to diminish the force of Dungy's remarks by drawing attention away from the substance of his objection and focusing instead on his personality.

But it is important to remember that Dungy didn't make any personal judgments about Ryan; he just said that Ryan shouldn't be cursing on television. He was objecting to a use of language that, once it becomes public, affects all of us by making our common world uglier. That's a significant objection, and worth taking seriously.

September 12, 2010

36. Playing the Game

"It's not whether you win or lose, it's how you play the game."

This particular saying is perhaps the best concise expression of the ethical attitude toward life.

Much of our culture's ethical wisdom is expressed in common folk sayings. The problem is, we repeat them to our children and to one another, but we don't take them seriously enough for ourselves. We use them to fill gaps in our conversation, but not as serious moral principles.

Ethics consists mainly of various constraints or limits we place upon ourselves in pursuit of our goals. I want to use my neighbor's lawn mower, but I must ask his permission first. I want to avoid embarrassment, but I must not tell a lie to do so. Without ethical constraints we would still have life, but we wouldn't have a life as rich and meaningful as it could be, because we wouldn't have friendship and community.

Chief among the constraints we place upon ourselves is that we must treat one another with respect. We may refer to this constraint by different names: "tolerance," "civilty," "manners," "politeness," "regard." But whatever we call it, it means basically the same thing: I should treat you the way that I would like to be treated. I should not attempt to cheat, mislead, manipulate, coerce, or belittle you in order to get something I want, no matter how important that something seems to be at the time.

The reason for this is fairly clear in some instances. For example, if I cheat in a round of golf by not counting a couple of penalty strokes on the scorecard, I may win some temporary satisfaction from the immediate outcome, but in the long run I have harmed my own character by not being trustworthy, and I have impaired a relationship that will now never reach its full potential.

The real challenge is to remember the importance of treating others with respect when the stakes are high, when it seems like there is nothing more important than the goal before me at this moment, whether that is closing an important business deal, passing a piece of legislation that will save the environment, or getting a ticket to the Packers-Vikings game.

At times like this it is important to remember that the long term outcome of events is rarely as clear cut in real life as it is in a ball game, that what seems like a victory at noon may have the appearance of defeat by evening. But the long term effect of treating others with respect is a gradual increase in mutual trust, and that continues to pay off throughout one's lifetime.

November 8, 2009

37. APOLOGY

I was looking to rent a power washer, and ended up finding a small shop in a block of mostly empty storefronts in downtown Memphis. The owner was one of those characters who is hard to forget.

He had been robbed several times at gunpoint, and his skulled fractured earlier in the year by a young man wielding an iron pipe. But what really worried him was the legal system. "I can't afford the insurance that the big chain stores carry," he said. "I'm just waiting for the day when a lawsuit shuts me down."

He went on to tell stories of customers determined to injure themselves with his equipment, like the guy who leaned an extension ladder upside down against his house and fell ten feet when he stepped onto the upper section of the ladder. He did that three times before coming back to the shop. "There's something wrong with this damn ladder!" he shouted.

"Every time somebody rents a piece of equipment, I go through how to use it. But most people don't pay attention or they do dumb things I would never even think of. Just ain't no cure for stupid," the shop owner concluded.

When things go wrong, our tendency is to create rules to prevent them from happening again. Then we hire experts to remind us what the rules are, how to interpret them, and how to protect ourselves from those who want to use the rules against us. We have lots of rules about how to use the rules.

One of the rules about rules is this: When somebody is injured, never say "I'm sorry"; it could be used against you in court.

Two Wisconsin legislators have introduced a bill to allow doctors to apologize to patients without fearing that the statement could be used against them in a lawsuit. The Wisconsin Medical Society and the Wisconsin Hospital Association support the bill; the Wisconsin Association for Justice (representing trial lawyers) opposes it.

What I have read of arguments on both sides seems fundamentally misguided. What bothers me about the debate is the assumption that whenever something goes wrong doctors and patients must necessarily become adversaries. It is an assumption in direct contradiction to the ethos of health care. It erodes the trust and confidence of the patient and undermines the morale of the health care worker.

Regardless of whether the bill passes, it doesn't have to be that way.

When Ken Melrose was CEO of Toro, he changed the way the company responded to customers injured by their products. Lawn mowers and snow blowers are inherently dangerous. No matter how safe Toro made their machines, some people still got injured. The challenge was how to respond.

Instead of seeking to change liability laws, they developed something called "Alternate Dispute Resolution." Whenever someone was injured using one of their products, regardless of whether they thought they might be at fault, they sent a team to investigate and—this is the crucial part—express their remorse.

Toro went from an average of 100 lawsuits a year, with half of them ending up in court, to settling two-thirds of their cases in the home and using a mediator for the rest. In the first 15 years of the program, only 1 injury case went to court.

Laws designed to protect consumers can sometimes cause even more harm by turning people who want to do the right thing into the enemy. But as the Toro example shows, we don't necessarily have to change the laws before we change our behavior.

People do stupid things, and sometimes those stupid things have terrible consequences. Most people understand that and are willing to make allowances, but only if goodwill and sincerity are evident at the outset.

The shop owner in Memphis could take heart from Toro's example. You don't have to be a large company to afford good customer service, and that turns out to be the best protection against lawsuits.

We shape our relationships by the conversations we have. And no healthy relationship can survive without the words, "I'm sorry."

April 7, 2013

38. PROGRESS

A popular series of television ads by Liberty Mutual shows people doing small acts of kindness, which in turn influence others to do similar acts. The ads are powerful because they remind us how easily goodness is spread, from one person to another, one action at a time.

But if goodness is so easily spread, why isn't there more of it? Why doesn't the world get better and better with each succeeding generation?

In the nineteenth century there was widespread belief in progress. Following the industrial and scientific revolutions, and the rise of capitalist economies, most people believed that progress in every area of life was inevitable.

World War I, however, shook confidence in the inevitability of moral progress, and World War II brought even more discouragement, not only due to the size of the conflict but the immensity of evil perpetrated by "civilized" nations like Germany.

The disparity between humanity's technological and moral progress led Will Rogers to quip, "You can't say civilization don't advance—for in every war, they kill you in a new way." Albert Einstein, looking back on his role in developing the atomic bomb, expressed the same idea, noting wryly that "technological progress is like an axe in the hands of a pathological criminal."

Things haven't changed much since World War II. Between 1945 and 2011 there were over 260 major armed conflicts around the world, mostly civil wars. Global violence reached a peak in 1992 with 51 simultaneous armed conflicts. By 2010 there were only 12 armed conflicts taking place, but the number increased again last year. The dream of a sustained period of world peace has been largely abandoned—as has every other utopian dream in the past 2,000 years.

Given all the great minds who have written about ethics, and all the great leaders who have dedicated themselves to reducing wars, ending child abuse, promoting equality, enhancing freedom, and encouraging civility, one would expect the world to be a better place than it is. If we can make progress in the areas of science and technology, why can't we make moral progress as well?

One reason is the fact that science is a cumulative exercise: each generation starts with the knowledge bequeathed to it by the previous generation. Newton, having described the law of gravity in the *Principia* in 1687, allowed others to pick up from there and advance the study of physics. Ethics, by contrast, is not cumulative, but cyclical. Each generation must start anew, discovering for themselves whether the insights, lessons, rules, and guidance passed down to them are worth retaining.

Another reason is that science requires the full participation of only a small percentage of the population. The Salk vaccine can prevent polio simply by being injected into people; the recipients don't have to know what is in it or how it functions; they don't even have to believe it will work. But ethics, in order to have significant effects in society, must be understood and agreed upon by a critical mass of the population.

A third reason is that science advances by experimentation, but ethics by presence. In science errors are corrected through trial and error, and once truth is established, it stays established. But ethics is passed along from one person to another on the basis of trust. If trust is broken, it can take years or even an entire generation to rebuild. Trust is a fragile condition in society, a condition that must be continually nurtured by each individual. It cannot be established once and for all.

Permanent moral progress may not be possible, but moral improvement is. Each individual, each family, each community, has opportunities to become better, by attending to mutual needs, often acting in little ways that encourage others to join in a conspiracy of goodness.

In this way each generation does what is theirs to do. And even though our actions do not ensure a lasting good, they can contribute to the common good, painstakingly cultivated in each new child who enters the world, bringing that child into a safe and loving circle of family, friends, and community, so that the same process may start all over again with the next generation.

January 29, 2012

POLITICS

39. DEMOCRACY

When I was a teenager I believed that by the time I was in my twenties I would know what to think about complicated social and political issues that seemed at the time to be completely baffling. I gave adults a great deal of credit for knowing things like who to vote for in political elections and what position to take on matters like war and economics.

When I reached my twenties I realized that things were more complicated than I had imagined, and that what I really wanted to know was why so many people thought they knew the answers to questions that were so impossibly difficult.

Now, at the age of forty-eight, I still don't know what position to take on most complicated matters such as war, economics, and health care. If pressed, I would venture an opinion that our troops should probably stay in Afghanistan for a while longer, that the economic stimulus package was probably a good thing overall, that health care reform legislation is both necessary and seriously flawed. But I am ready to be persuaded otherwise. Every election year I am pressed to vote for a candidate, but I have rarely voted for someone without doubts or misgivings. I am resigned to living with such uncertainty for the rest of my life.

What continues to perplex me is the number of people who are not resigned to uncertainty. How can they possibly know what they claim to know? And how can they get so angry with people who disagree with them?

In Ralph Waldo Emerson's "Experience" he expresses a skeptical mood which is sometimes thought to be uncharacteristic of him, but which is recurrent in his later writings. He says:

> I have not found that much was gained by manipular attempts to realize the world of thought. Many ea-

ger persons successively make an experiment in this way, and make themselves ridiculous. They acquire democratic manners, they foam at the mouth, they hate and deny.... [But] the results of life are uncalculated and uncalculable. The years teach much which the days never know. The persons who compose our company converse, and come and go, and design and execute many things, and somewhat comes of it all, but an unlooked-for result. The individual is always mistaken.

Over the years I have changed my mind on just about every major social issue, and I expect that I may change my mind again about several of them. I have serious political disagreements with good friends, neighbors, and family members, people whom I love and respect. And though I wish I were wiser and more informed about important issues, I also cannot help thinking that our shared ignorance about matters of vital significance is, in the end, a good thing. It keeps us humble, and mutually dependent upon one another.

Winston Churchill is reported to have said during a speech in the House of Commons: "No one pretends that democracy is perfect or all-wise. Indeed, it has been said that democracy is the worst form of government except all those other forms that have been tried from time to time."

Perhaps the great virtue of democracy is its very inefficiency, which rewards patience, persistence, and cooperation. It forces us always to turn back towards one another, even to those we disagree with most strongly, and find ways of working things out—once again.

November 7, 2010

40. The Character of Politicians

It is rare to find people today who are satisfied with the state of politics in our society. Whether we hear complaints about the lack of civility among elected officials, behind-the-scenes deal-making, partisan posturing, or negative campaigning, the most frequently heard remarks about politics are overwhelmingly negative.

And yet, nearly everyone is quick to defend democracy as the best form of government. In fact, any visitor just arriving in America during an election year would be quick to observe that we love our form of government, yet we despise our politicians.

Even the politicians that we most admire in our history books were not universally admired in their own time. Consider, for example, George Washington. Most Americans today would agree that, regardless of other limitations he may have had, he was certainly a person of integrity. There is, of course, the story of the cherry tree. But there are also other examples noted by historians: his thoroughgoing insistence on independence—his own independence from political parties and the country's independence from foreign nations; and, also, his decision not to seek a third term in office, which set the precedent for smooth transfer of political power.

Washington's critics, however, attacked him precisely for lacking the characteristic we regard as most definitive of his career. His fellow revolutionary, Thomas Paine, wrote to him: "the world will be puzzled to decide whether you are an apostate or an imposter, whether you have abandoned good principles, or whether you ever had any."

One of the chief problems facing politicians in a democracy is that they must take public positions on issues that are not only highly charged and difficult to resolve, but often insoluble.

By the very nature of their office politicians cannot rest with ambiguity on issues that are socially divisive: abortion, gun control, taxes, environmental regulation, stem cell research, foreign trade policies, health care reform. Private citizens, however, have the advantage of choosing when and where they will share their views on such issues. We have the option, if we wish, of avoiding the difficult issues and limiting our conversations to those topics that are politically neutral—like fishing, the weather, the Green Bay Packers—or restricting our conversation about politically controversial topics to the people we know will agree with us.

Politicians do not have that luxury. Not only do they have to express their views publicly, they have to do so in a practical fashion—by passing laws, enforcing policies, and rendering judgments—that may seriously impact our lives. This situation ensures that most people will have several good reasons to dislike most politicians most of the time.

The politicians we admire from our nation's past are probably more like the politicians of the present age than we would like to admit. The "founding fathers" had more character flaws than our history books record, and today's politicians have more virtues than we read about in the press. From my own limited experience I can say that the politicians I have had the privilege of knowing have been, on the whole, among the brightest, hardest-working, and sincerest people I've ever met.

That shouldn't keep us from disagreeing with them strongly when the occasion warrants, but it should cause us to remember that we are asking them to do a nearly impossible job, and that they are probably acting in much the same way that we would in their place.

December 6, 2009

41. DISAPPOINTMENT

Shortly after the presidential election, I talked with a young man who was distraught over the outcome. He had convinced himself that Mitt Romney would win, and it was difficult for him to acknowledge that voters had selected the person who seemed to him the worse candidate. His disappointment expressed a sincere belief that America would be permanently harmed by continuation of President Obama's foreign and domestic policies and fear that his own prospects for a successful life would be diminished.

It is easy for those on the winning side to discount the disappointment of those on the losing side. It is easy, but unwise; for when the voting population is closely divided between two parties, it is likely that most voters will be disappointed much of the time. This means that we are all faced, on a regular basis, with the question of how we should respond to the frustration of our political hopes.

Hopes and fears are based on what we imagine the future will be like.

Most of us rely upon experts to tell us what the future will be like in complex areas of life, for example, world conflict, stock market, jobs.

For the most part, the experts are mistaken.

We rely upon our own judgment to predict whether we will be positively or negatively affected by how things turn out.

For the most part, we are mistaken.

Philip Tetlock, a psychologist at the University of Pennsylvania, studies how experts make predictions. In his book, *Expert Political Judgment,* he demonstrates that experts are no better than the average informed citizen at predicting future outcomes. Moreover, the better known experts, those who are most often interviewed on radio and television and quoted in the newspapers, are even more likely to be wrong than those who are less well known.

But we are not only poor predictors of future events, we are also quite poor at predicting how we will respond emotionally to those events. Daniel Gilbert, author of *Stumbling on Happiness*, studied two groups of people, those who won a state lottery and those who lost the use of both legs in an accident. He discovered that just one year after the event, both groups of people returned to the approximate level of happiness that they had before those events.

A century before the advent of modern empirical psychology, Emerson, in the essay "Experience," noted that "we do not see directly, but mediately, and that we have no means of correcting these colored and distorting lenses which we are, or of computing the amount of their errors."

Daniel Kahneman, author of *Thinking, Fast and Slow,* and winner of the Nobel Prize in Economics, has amassed decades of evidence showing that even though we all believe that our decisions are based on rational deliberation, that belief is just another example of pervasive wishful thinking. Our judgments are nearly always less reliable than we think they are.

After the Shay's Rebellion of 1787, Thomas Jefferson wrote a letter to James Madison, advising him to be patient, not to overreact. Jefferson understood that our emotional response to events is generally unwarranted, and that democracy depends on our willingness to work through difficulties together, even in the face of serious disagreements. He said, "those characters wherein fear predominates over hope...may conclude too hastily that nature has formed man insusceptible of any other government than that of force, a conclusion which is not founded in truth, nor experience."

None of this means that it doesn't matter who wins an election, or what judges are appointed, or what laws are passed. It certainly does matter, though precisely how it matters often isn't evident until years later, when we have a chance to look back over the history of events and draw lines of causation from decisions to results.

What it does mean is that we are never justified in wronging one another for the sake of a future which may or may not come to pass. We are never justified in deceiving, manipulating, or coercing our fellow citizens for the sake of political gain. To do so is to exchange an uncertain benefit for a known harm.

December 16, 2012

42. Social Capital

When Governor Scott Walker delivered the State of the State address in January, his chief focus was on the economy. That's understandable. We elect governors to be stewards of public institutions, and we expect them to oversee the responsible use of tax revenues and to advance wise and fair policies that foster economic health. We judge their performance primarily on that basis.

But the economy is not the only determinant of a healthy society. A more important indicator, though harder to measure, is social capital.

Social capital is what allows a democracy to flourish. It consists of the ways in which citizens interact with one another, creating collaborative networks that advance the common good. Social capital is generated whenever citizens gather together in some sort of shared enterprise. Churches, service organizations, schools, libraries, book clubs, rod and gun clubs, neighborhood taverns, festivals, sporting leagues—all contribute to the health of society by fostering social capital.

But social capital is a threatened resource in America. In 2000, Harvard sociologist Robert Putnam published *Bowling Alone,* a book that documented the steady decline in civic engagement over the latter half of the 20th century. Numerous reasons were given for the decline, including demographic shifts from rural to urban communities and the prevalence of electronic media. But regardless of the cause, the results were clear: Americans are retreating from public life and becoming increasingly private.

(An interesting side note: the term "idiot" comes from an ancient Greek term meaning "private person." The Greeks, who devised the democratic form of government, thought failure to participate fully in some form of public life could only come from inability, not free choice.)

Social capital comes in two forms: bonding capital and bridging capital. Bonding capital results when friends and acquaintances get together to share mutual interests. Bridging capital results when people from diverse backgrounds and identities come together for a common purpose. While bonding capital is important, a society's ability to create and sustain bridging capital is the primary indicator of health and resiliency.

We have many opportunities in Wisconsin for bonding capital. Service organizations, churches, and sporting leagues, for example, do a great job of bringing like-minded people out of their homes and into a shared public space. But bridging capital is more difficult to achieve. Our schools and public festivals are the chief places where large numbers of people from different races, social classes, and political affinities come together on a regular basis.

Government does not create social capital, but it depends upon it in order to function effectively.

In a democratic society, lasting good can only be produced by consensus. When a political faction uses its power to leverage policies that do not have popular support, the immediate results are generally short-lived. The long term results are public cynicism and political upheaval.

Consensus building requires trust, which is produced by social capital. No social capital, no trust. No trust, no consensus. No consensus, no political stability. No political stability, no lasting good.

We know from business that if employees are arguing with each other, they provide lousy customer service. Basketball teams that do not communicate on the floor have losing records. Surgical teams that do not talk with each other have more negative outcomes. Why do we suppose that the people we elect can dislike one another and still do a good job of governing?

How can we expect the people who represent us in government to get along if we don't get along in our own communities? And how can we get along if we don't know one another?

We can complain about the state of politics in Madison, but the root of the problem is at home. If we want better politics, there is an obvious place to start. It is by asking the question: what am I doing to enhance social capital in my community? After all, if the state of our communities is healthy, the state of the State will follow.

February 26, 2012

43. The Common Good

On June 5, the Congressional Budget Office released its Long-Term Budget Outlook. It predicts that the federal debt will reach 70% of gross domestic product (GDP) by the end of the year, a level not reached since World War II.

But that's not the really bad news; the really bad news is that if we keep postponing practical solutions, the debt could reach 200% by 2037. Projecting budget trends for the next 25 years, the CBO concludes: "Policymakers will need to increase revenues substantially above historical levels as a percentage of GDP, decrease spending significantly from projected levels, or adopt some combination of those two approaches."

In other words, the government will have to increase taxes and cut spending. The longer the government postpones action on these two fronts, the fewer options it will have in the future and the more drastic its actions will have to be.

Taking action on both fronts is made less likely by the rising influence of Grover Norquist and his Taxpayer Protection Pledge. The pledge itself is simple. It requires signers to "oppose any and all efforts to increase the marginal income tax rates for individuals and/or businesses."

Signers of the tax pledge fall for the most part along party lines. All but 13 Republican members of the House and Senate have signed the pledge; only 3 Democrats have signed it.

All citizens have an obligation to pay their fair share for the goods and services provided by the government. The question is: how much is a fair amount?

The Taxpayer Protection Pledge doesn't attempt to answer that question. It begins with the assumption that everyone is currently paying too much.

There are both economic and moral arguments for lowering taxes. The economic arguments are beyond my expertise, but the chief moral argument is that many (or even most) social services ought to be provided by the private sector instead of by government. Paying for government services through taxes is a form of coercion, while paying for services through the private sector respects individual freedom.

One way of looking at the debate over taxes is to note the subtle difference between the "common good" and the "greater good."

If it is government's role to advance the "common good," then it relies upon a vision of a flourishing life in which all citizens may share. In the words of the Catholic document *"Gaudium et Spes,"* "the common good [is] the sum of those conditions of social life which allow social groups and their individual members relatively thorough and ready access to their own fulfillment.... Therefore, there must be made available to all men everything necessary for leading a life truly human, such as food, clothing, and shelter."

On the other hand, if the role of government is to advance the "greater good," then its obligation is to provide a social and legal context within which the greatest number of citizens may reach optimal individual satisfaction. This way of thinking comes to us from Jeremy Bentham, the 18th century political reformer: "It is in vain to talk of the interest of the community, without understanding what is the interest of the individual."

I find both ideas compelling. I agree with advocates of the common good that investments in certain resources, like education, roads, parks, and health care, make life better for all of us in ways that would not be possible if left for us to pursue individually. On the other hand, I agree with advocates of the greater good that individuals have ultimate responsibility for themselves and that government assistance can be counterproductive if it doesn't respect the freedom of individuals to live (and spend their money) as they choose.

Both sides are in this debate are motivated by a vision of the good society, and yet the most vocal members tend to define themselves more by what they will not tolerate than by what they would be willing to sacrifice. The right doesn't want to raise taxes; the left doesn't want to cut services. And yet both sides will have to give up some of what they think is good in order to do what's right for the next generation.

July 15, 2012

44. POLITICAL FALLACIES

Just weeks before the presidential election in 1984, Aunt Eva swallowed the last bit of her egg salad sandwich and added her two cents to the discussion taking place around the table: "I could never vote for Mondale," she said with casual conviction, "he looks like a frog."

This was to be my first time voting, and I admit my enthusiasm for going to the polls took a direct hit. What do you say to someone who reasons like that and seems perfectly happy about it? How many similarly ill-reasoned citizens will show up on Election Day to cast their ballot? If that's how elections are decided, what's the point of voting?

The truth is that we all reason like that occasionally. Careful, deliberate reasoning is hard work, and despite the fact that nearly everyone agrees society would be improved by more critical thinking, few of us acknowledge that the practice should begin with ourselves.

Faulty reasoning falls into identifiable patterns, known as logical fallacies. Fallacies are common because they provide simple shortcuts to conclusions that affirm our assumptions and prejudices, and most of us would rather be affirmed than be informed.

Learning to identify some of the more common fallacies can be particularly helpful during an election year.

Perhaps the most frequently employed is the "straw man" fallacy, so called because it consists of putting forth a false representation of an opponent's position in order to refute it. For example, to say that Democrats just want to tax hard-working citizens and give their money to freeloaders is an example of the straw man fallacy. It is easy to dismiss such a policy as bad economics, but then, nobody, including Democrats, would seriously try to defend it. Generally speaking, anyone who suggests that a candidate's position on an issue is just downright dumb is guilty of the straw man fallacy. Politicians may sometimes say dumb things—and there have been several notable incidents of dumb remarks in the past few months—but their positions on issues tend to be carefully considered and rationally defensible.

Another common fallacy is the false dilemma. It consists of holding that there are only two possible alternatives to an issue when in reality there are several. For instance, claiming that one must choose between raising taxes and cutting spending is a false dilemma. A sound economic policy will consider many options, including the complicated matters of tax reform, changing the fee-for-service reimbursement in Medicare, job creation strategies, etc. A good rule of thumb: generally when someone says "the choice is clear," it's not.

A third common fallacy is the *ad hominem*. This fallacy consists of attacking the person delivering the message rather than criticizing the message itself. It is a fallacy because what a person says should usually be evaluated independently of who the person is. This fallacy can take several forms, from outright name calling, to labeling policies after their proponents (like calling health care reform "Obamacare"), to rejecting a candidate because he looks like a frog.

We rely upon fallacies because they allow us to assume the appearance of certainty without doing the hard work of backing up our assertions. We should know better. Constant certainty is a sure sign of ignorance. And yet, we rarely encourage one another to ask difficult questions, nor do we reward politicians for doing so. A politician who really does listen and changes his or her mind as a result is regarded as "indecisive" or a "flip-flopper."

Political campaigns encourage the use of fallacies. Whereas good governance requires careful listening, effective campaigning requires persistent criticism of the opponent. Once politics turns into perpetual campaigning, public discussion about how we ought to live together, what laws and policies should be enacted, what procedures are fair and just, become contests between winners and losers rather than honest deliberations about the common good.

It is not the responsibility of politicians alone to respect the difference between campaigning and governing. It is primarily the responsibility of ordinary citizens. We have to ensure that in our own discussions with one another we pay attention to the truth, ask serious questions, and neither participate in nor fall prey to fallacious rhetoric.

October 7, 2012

45. ATTACK ADS

Over the past several weeks I've heard numerous discussions about why the political climate in Wisconsin and the nation has become so contentious. One explanation comes up over and over again. "The main reason," someone will say," is that Citizens United allows outside interest groups to spend huge sums of money on political attack ads."

The explanation refers to the U.S. Supreme Court case Citizens United v. Federal Election commission, a 5–4 ruling which declared certain provisions of the McCain-Feingold Act unconstitutional. In the year since the decision, there has been a noticeable increase in TV and radio ads just before elections, funded by special interest groups, most of them negative in content and tone. But is this really why the political climate is so contentious?

Justice Kennedy, who authored the majority opinion in Citizens United, wrote that curtailing campaign ads would run the "serious risk of chilling protected speech" and, quoting Justice Roberts, argued that First Amendment standards "must give the benefit of any doubt to protecting rather than stifling speech."

The majority opinion is certainly correct in noting that the First Amendment was intended to protect political speech. And whatever one thinks about the societal effects of unregulated campaign ads, one must admit that they constitute political speech.

But it is important to note that campaign ads are a mode of speech that proves more effective at tearing down than building up.

For any issue, whether it is global climate change, economic reform, education funding, or agricultural policies, to make one's position seem reasonable takes careful and detailed explanation. But to make the same position seem ridiculous can generally be done with just one artfully crafted phrase.

This is the case not just with political issues, but with almost anything we do: "Golf is the sport of chasing a little white ball." "Fishing is just sitting in a boat waving a stick." "Bankers steal from the poor and give to the rich." "Farming is the art of harvesting subsidies from taxpayers." "Those who can't do, teach."

The problem with using words to ridicule people and activities is that it is possible to make anything we do—anything we care about—appear foolish.

We saw the outcome of the politics of ridicule in the recent debt-limit negotiations on Capitol Hill. When politicians are elected by belittling their opposition, the result is that any compromise implies a willingness to make concessions to fools. Yet, compromise is the heart of politics. It is the only way democracies get things done.

To engage in compromise requires that one see the possibility of merit in the opposition's view. That such merit is always a possibility is actually the justification for free speech in the first place.

Consider the words of Learned Hand, a staunch defender of free speech and widely regarded as one of America's greatest jurists: "The spirit of liberty is the spirit which is not too sure that it is right; the spirit of liberty is the spirit which seeks to understand the mind of other men and women; the spirit of liberty is the spirit which weighs their interests alongside its own without bias."

James Madison, who penned the Bill of Rights, understood that free speech should be a constitutional right, not because all speech is morally permissible, but because government should not be the sole arbiter of moral permissibility.

Madison believed that citizens themselves must take seriously the obligation to monitor their own speech. He wrote: "Is there no virtue among us? If there be not, we are in a wretched situation. No theoretical checks—no form of government can render us secure. To suppose liberty or happiness without any virtue in the people, is a chimerical idea."

If negative campaign ads are having a corrosive effect on our nation's politics, it is not because the Supreme Court protects them. It is because we citizens are not vigorously defending true freedom, by supporting the organizations that fund corrosive speech and electing the politicians that benefit from it.

Corrosive speech is part of what is protected by the First Amendment. But that doesn't mean it is ethically defensible. It doesn't mean we should meekly accept it as something worth listening to.

August 28, 2011

46. Hyperbole

The other day I received a mass email from a political group looking for support. "They're at it again!" it declared. "This vote could overturn years of hard fought gains!" But "there's still time to act." "Call your legislators now."

The problem is, most of what the message claimed was false, or at least grossly exaggerated.

So instead of calling my legislators I called the offices of the political group responsible for the email. A young man answered the phone. We had a pleasant conversation during which I patiently pointed out the inaccuracies in the email. To my surprise, he acknowledged that the email was "less than accurate." However, he continued, "we need to do this to engage our base."

And that, in a nutshell, is the cause of many people's frustration with party politics.

One of Aesop's better known fables is about the boy who cried "wolf!" The boy was a shepherd who enjoyed watching the townsfolk come running whenever he yelled out his warning. And he had much cause for amusement, until a wolf actually did appear and no one paid attention to him.

Political advocacy groups have devised increasingly effective ways of getting people's attention, but not of keeping it. And that's because they are so committed to the urgency of their message that they don't practice the self-restraint necessary to become trustworthy.

Most people working for political advocacy groups believe in the message they are delivering. They think the city or county or state or nation or world will be a better place if their agenda is enacted. Whether they are concerned about polluted lakes, unborn children, increasing debt, unemployment, education, or health care, they are sincere. They are not cynical or simple-minded or self-interested. They are intelligent, well-informed, and passionate.

And they are consequentialists.

To be a consequentialist is to care more about the goal one is striving to achieve than about the means one takes to achieve it. But to be trustworthy requires telling the truth, even when it is contrary to one's own interest. Even if it makes it harder to achieve one's goals.

Immanuel Kant, the 18th century Prussian philosopher, was famous for his criticism of consequentialism. This found expression in his prohibition against lying—which included any form of exaggeration, omission, or hyperbole—any attempt, that is, to use words to mislead people.

Why did he think lying was so bad? Because words are the instruments of reason, and it is reason that allows us to discern what is good and to act willingly upon it. Words, in short, are the means by which we are able to act ethically. And if we use words to deceive, we not only commit a wrong, we deprive others of the ability to make informed ethical choices. We deprive them of the opportunity to use their full human capacities.

I confess I have not always found Kant's arguments for truth-telling convincing. But recently, as I've reflected on the political groups that seem willing to say anything to "get their message across," I've begun to see the wisdom of Kant's words.

Without honesty, all we have is manipulation. And even well-intentioned manipulation, though it may attain good short-term goals, inevitably results in cynicism and despair. It deprives us all of a common language which we may use to find shared solutions to problems, to create a better society.

Truth is not a private possession; it is a common good. It is not up to me to decide whether I will speak truly or falsely, for words, once uttered, become common property. If uttered falsely, they become a common burden, like a polluted stream that someone, somewhere, must clean up, or it will continue to afflict everyone who comes in contact with it.

Tell the truth and tell it simply. That should be the first commandment of anyone who takes part in politics.

August 14, 2011

RELIGION

47. IMPOSING RELIGION

Sometimes an expression gains currency in society and people begin repeating it without stopping to think about whether it makes sense. That is the case with the expression "imposing religion."

Think of all the things we impose in our society: taxes, seatbelts, building codes, pet vaccinations, air pollution, loud noises, processed foods, pasteurized milk, advertisements, popular music. If we tried to make a list of all the things most imposed upon us in the course of our daily lives, I doubt whether religion would make it into the top one hundred.

Of course, people occasionally have uncomfortable experiences with others who are obstinate and insensitive in talking about their religious beliefs. But we also encounter any number of people who are overly pushy about their political, or economic, or environmental beliefs. I've never felt that such people were "imposing" their beliefs on me; I have, however, often felt that such people were rude and mistaken.

Most organized religions in our country go out of their way not to impose their beliefs and practices upon even their own membership, much less the general public. Churches are voluntary associations. They have to attract and retain members through invitation, not coercion. If they get too pushy, people leave. If a pastor preaches a sermon that is longer than usual, he hears about it immediately after the service. If a denominational hierarchy makes a decision that is unpopular, members of congregations leave or reduce their donations.

The majority of mission trips that are sponsored by U.S. churches today are not done for the sake of converting others. In fact, it's just the opposite. Most mission trips are intended to take churchgoers out of the comfort and safety of their lives into a place where they can be open to the experience of the divine without the distractions and supports that make up much of their daily lives. Teenagers go from a church in La Crosse to a village in rural Appalachia to help fix houses; they find their own faith awakened by the music and prayers of the people they are serving. A medical mission team goes to Haiti and learns from the Haitians how to have faith in the face of catastrophe.

What about when people vote or support legislation on the basis of their religious beliefs? Surely that is imposing religion upon others! Well, I'm not so sure. All of us try to influence public policy in one way or another based on our ethical views— what we think is right or wrong. And we have many sources for those views, including scientific, medical, economic, political, and educational outlooks. It would be an odd thing to say, for example, "You can vote for a candidate based on your belief in capitalism, but not based on your belief in providence."

We normally agree that our main concern in democracy is with the process for determining political outcomes, and we are willing to allow people to believe anything they want as long as they agree to fair rules of participation. I suspect part of the reason for using the phrase "imposing religion" is that it makes resistance to religious ideas a matter of process rather than truth. And claims about process have an intrinsic weight in our democratic culture.

But the real opposition to religious beliefs comes from people who think that they are false and therefore provide a poor basis for any kind of decision—especially decisions affecting public life. There is something to be said for this. We can be fairly confident that many religious beliefs are false, just as many widely held historical, scientific, and political beliefs are false. But that doesn't get us anywhere. We still have to look at our beliefs one at a time: ask questions about them, find out where they came from, what their implications are, and where they will lead us.

None of us likes to be "imposed upon." We want to be treated by our fellow citizens with respect, consideration, and civility. That's something we can all agree upon, no matter where we fall on the religious divide. Or would that be imposing the Golden Rule?

March 21, 2010

48. Consumption

I confess to not understanding much of the contemporary debate over the relationship between ethics and religion. Most of the criticisms I read of "religion" are simply echoes of disputes that have been taking place within theological circles for centuries.

If a person criticizes Christians for irrationally believing that the earth was created in six twenty-four hour days, well, there are many Catholics and Protestants who would agree, beginning with St. Augustine. If someone points out that people who go to church do bad things, that's hardly news. Jesus, after all, said he came "not to call the righteous, but sinners to repentance." (A more pertinent criticism would be that churches have too many "good" people in them.)

Broad criticisms miss the mark because there is no consensus on what constitutes true ethics or true religion. To get to the interesting debate you have to address particular ideas, but once you get down to particular ideas, you can't draw general conclusions about "ethics" and "religion." You are instead immersed in the consideration of "this ethical principle," "this religious doctrine," and so on.

That's why I largely avoid the general debate and continue to look for wisdom wherever it can be found, whether those sources be religious or not, and whether they come from my own tradition or not.

Let me share an example. At this time of year I struggle, as many do, with the proper attitude to take towards shopping. Not wanting to succumb to the consumer frenzy that characterizes events like "black Friday" but wanting at the same time to be a grateful participant in the rituals of gift giving and receiving by which we demonstrate our love and concern for one another, I look for ways of making sense of my ambivalence toward the holidays. Then I recall this passage from *Centesimus Annus,* a Roman Catholic encyclical written in 1991 by Pope John Paul II:

> It is not wrong to want to live better: what is wrong is a style of life which is presumed to be better when it is directed towards "having" rather than "being," and which wants to have more, not in order to be more but in order to spend life in enjoyment as an end in itself. It is therefore necessary to create lifestyles in which the quest for truth, beauty, goodness and communion with others for the sake of common growth are the factors which determine consumer choices, savings and investments.

I find the Pope's words challenging and edifying. He articulates in a concise fashion what the problem is and points a way out of that problem. And the words acquire even greater significance in the context of the rest of the document, which goes on to describe the pervasiveness of soul-sickness, the human inclination to satisfy the thirst for meaning by acquiring possessions, which is not only ultimately unsatisfying but also detrimental to relationships and destructive to the environment.

The passage is "ethical" in its focus because it says something about how to live, and it is also "religious" in that it proceeds from a conception of human life as having a God-given purpose. I take the words seriously because they seem to me authoritative. Not in the sense that I must believe them (since I am not Catholic), but in the sense that they seem to be true (which is the highest kind of authority, the kind Matthew attributed to Jesus).

Does this mean that ethics is dependent upon religion? No, of course not. But I have to admit that my own understanding of ethics is frequently enhanced by reading people whose words are informed by a transcendent vision of the world. Such words help to pull me out of my narrow, self-interested focus and to look upward and outward toward the good for all. And that seems to me like a good thing.

December 5, 2010

49. JOY

Last week the Freedom from Religion Foundation objected to a nativity scene set up in the Wisconsin Capitol rotunda.

When disputes over the public display of religious imagery take place, it's natural for people who identify with the religion in question to feel under attack, that their way of life is somehow being taken away from them.

People outside of the religious tradition tend to feel under attack as well, as if their group lacks political legitimacy.

And so the holidays become an occasion for division rather than unity, and the participants in the battles become so myopic that they fail to see the bigger picture. The fights over who gets to display what, and where, and when, and how become petty and even ridiculous.

Recently a grade school teacher in Virginia was told to take down a cut-out paper Christmas tree with the names of her students inscribed upon it. Someone was offended by the display's heading, which read "Santa's Little Helpers."

There is no danger that Santa Claus will end up as a casualty of the culture wars. He's too substantial a figure in commercial iconography for that to happen. But what could be lost is the religious language that provides a meaningful contrast to the kind of happiness that Santa provides.

That could happen, not through court battles over public displays, but through simple inattention, through neglect of the songs, prayers, and stories with which participants in religious traditions have been entrusted.

Religious language is meaningful because it helps us to understand ourselves and the world better. Words are the bearers of inherited meaning; they provide us with possibilities, ways of seeing things differently, which result in ways of living differently.

But when a word is forgotten, the meaning it carried is forgotten as well. A certain way of making sense of the world and our experience in it is lost.

Take the word "joy," for example. The notion of joy is central to the Christian understanding of the good life, and the Advent season (or days leading up to Christmas) is the time when joy is the characteristic expression.

Joy is just one of a number of words connoting a mode of happiness, along with words like satisfaction, fulfillment, and gratification. But joy is distinctive. C. S. Lewis, in one of his letters, writes: "All joy (as distinct from mere pleasure, still more amusement) emphasizes our pilgrim status; always reminds, beckons, awakens desire. Our best havings are wantings."

Joy is an emotion in which time itself is transformed, when we move from time as *chronos* (measured time) to time as *kairos* (meaningful time). To speak of the fourth Sunday of Advent is to speak in terms of *kairos*—a time of preparation and anticipation. To talk about six shopping days left until Christmas is to speak in terms of *chronos*—a series of days checked off the calendar.

Nearly all of Christian ethics depends upon the distinctive experience of joy. Christians are pilgrims on a journey between here and there, and as such must look out for one another, providing as much charity, comfort, and encouragement as possible along the way. Time spent in this life will not be completely satisfying; in fact, some days will be devastating.

That's why joy is so significant. It's just the glimpse one gets now and then, and especially at certain times of the year, that life has more to offer than what each day brings.

Young children will always prefer Christmas morning to Advent. But as we get older we realize that anticipation is better than having, and that our fondest memories come from the times before the presents were opened. This is an important lesson for the rest of the year also—that time spent together, getting ready, caring for one another along the way, is when we experience joy.

Joy is a gift Santa can't bring down the chimney. And it can only be removed from the Capitol rotunda if Christians themselves forget to name it.

December 18, 2011

50. EVOLUTION

Last month the state of Tennessee passed legislation to protect teachers at public high schools who question the scientific evidence for evolution. Defenders of the legislation insist it simply protects "academic freedom." Critics claim it will allow creationism to be taught in science classes.

The evolution-creation debate is profound. It invites reflection upon the most basic questions of human existence. Unfortunately, the people driving the debate seem to be those least capable of understanding its significance.

In fact, the evolution-creation debate is one of those rare instances where the majority of people on both sides are seriously misguided.

The advocates of creationism are mistaken in thinking that the problem with evolutionary theory lies in the inadequacy of scientific evidence supporting it.

But many defenders of evolution have been irresponsible in claiming that natural selection can explain not only biological development, but all aspects of human culture, including ethics.

If one begins with the assumption that all ways of understanding the world other than the scientific mode of thinking are irrelevant, then of course one will think that the only good explanations are scientific ones. But that is an assumption entirely unsupportable by scientific evidence. It requires a philosophical argument.

A case in point is Stephen Hawking, who, at a conference last year, made the observation that "almost all of us must sometimes wonder: Why are we here? Where do we come from? Traditionally, these are questions for philosophy, but philosophy is dead." Hawking believes only science can answer the fundamental questions of human existence. The problem is, that itself is a philosophical belief, not a scientific one.

One way to understand the difference between science and philosophy is to reflect that there are two basic types of explanation: causes and reasons. Scientific explanations deal with causes, which explain how things happen. Philosophical explanations deal with reasons, which explain why things happen.

Because our language is ambiguous, it is not always clear whether we are talking about reasons or causes. For example, if I were to ask John why he kicked the cat, he could say "Because my leg twitched" (cause), or he could say "Because I hate cats" (reason). The science of physiology may explain what caused his leg to twitch, but it could not explain why he hates cats or whether his hatred of cats is a sufficient reason for kicking them. That simply requires a different type of explanation.

Consider the question "Is generosity a virtue?" It is possible to give a scientific answer explaining the survival advantage of various character traits, but that would not give anyone a reason to be generous. It would just explain how the belief came about.

It is bad science to claim that evolution cannot explain biological development, and it is bad philosophy to claim that evolution can explain ethics. The evidence in support of natural selection is overwhelming, but natural selection does not explain everything that is important about human life, for example, why it is wrong to kick cats and good to be generous.

Because science and philosophy employ different kinds of explanation, they have different criteria for determining truth and falsity. But since creationists are infatuated with scientific reasoning, they are unwilling to acknowledge that non-scientific claims may be (literally) true, and so they insist that a proper understanding of human nature can be obtained only in the science classroom. The result is that there is no place within the public school curriculum to suitably address the basic question that underpins all of ethics: what gives life meaning?

The real tragedy is that neither side in the debate appreciates the creation story for what it really has to offer: genuine insight into the reasons for human existence. By insisting that the evolution-creation debate is only about science both sides ensure that the fundamental questions about human purpose will never be answered to anyone's satisfaction.

The members of the Tennessee legislature may be correct in thinking that there is something wrong with the content of public education, but their solution just makes the problem worse.

What we really need is some basic education in philosophical reasoning, beginning with those who wish to influence school curriculum.

May 20, 2012

51. Traditional Morality

Is traditional morality obsolete?

According to Harvard University education professor Howard Gardner it is. In a recent *New York Times* opinion piece titled "Reinventing Ethics" he argued that the world has become too large and complex for the moral codes devised for small localized communities: "As I see it, human beings and citizens in complex, modern democratic societies regularly confront situations in which traditional morality provides little if any guidance."

Gardner is not the only one saying this. The world is changing, and our understanding of the world is advancing along with those changes. The idea that ethics must change as the world changes is commonplace.

But many critics of traditional morality base their criticisms on a misunderstanding which Gardner shares. "If my argument is correct," he writes, "the professional deals every day with issues that cannot possibly be decided simply by consulting the Bible or some other traditional moral code."

To think that traditional morality consists of simplistic applications of prescriptions is itself a simplistic notion.

Despite what critics of the Christian gospels frequently claim, Jesus never says, "Follow these rules and you will be saved." Rather, he tells stories, he challenges religious authorities, and he questions his own followers, never allowing them to feel satisfied with their understanding of right and wrong.

Anyone who thinks the Bible provides moral certainty has not read it carefully.

One has only to notice how Jesus responds to the Pharisees, how the Apostle Paul writes to the church at Corinth, or how the rabbis interpret the Torah in the Talmud, to see that determining the right thing to do is not a simple exercise but requires humility, wisdom, and imagination.

To be fair to Gardner, it is true that technological developments present us with circumstances never encountered before. Once scientists mapped the human genome, the question of how to use this knowledge was raised for the first time. Such developments require new thinking, but they do not necessarily require us to abandon traditional concepts.

On the contrary, the more the world changes, the more important it is to recover the traditional concepts that our ancestors developed to meet the challenges of their changing world. We don't have to reinvent the wheel; we just have to figure out how to make it work on new roads.

Just because we cannot turn to Confucius or Aristotle for specific answers to contemporary moral dilemmas involving end-of-life decisions, or internet privacy, or genetic modifications does not mean that traditional moral sources are obsolete. Classical ethical texts endure because they deal with basic concepts which underlie and inform our understanding of how to live. In his letter to the Corinthians, for example, the Apostle Paul tried to explain why love is essential to human flourishing, not provide an exhaustive list of acceptable behaviors.

Whether it is the Bible, the *Bhagavad Gita,* or Plato's *Republic,* sources of traditional moral concepts are important because they remind us that certain ideas endure because they are grounded in fundamental insights into human nature. And even though technology, medicine, economics, and politics change over time, human nature stays pretty much the same.

Maybe that's why contemporary research into the conditions of human happiness confirms the central notions of traditional morality. The key contributors to happiness are a modest income and stable, committed relationships. In other words, obtaining an education, finding meaningful work, getting married, having children, being involved in the communi-ty: all these traditional activities tend to make a person happy.

What contributes to unhappiness? Pursuing wealth at the expense of family, having extramarital affairs, being self-indul-gent or suspicious, persistent gambling, drinking to excess, isolating oneself from others: anything that destroys relation-ships.

It turns out the Apostle Paul was right: love really is the greatest virtue because more than anything else it character-izes healthy relationships. And the seven deadly sins really are deadly—they destroy relationships, and therefore make us (and those around us) miserable.

The most recent, sophisticated research on happiness has not provided us with new answers to life's persistent questions; it has merely confirmed the age-old answers. So instead of con-stantly trying to change morality to fit what society has become, maybe we should look again at the traditional moral sources to learn how to change ourselves.

February 10, 2013

52. OTHER CULTURES

One of the challenging things about living in a global society is that we frequently hear about practices in other countries that seem to us strange—or even morally outrageous. An example is the case of Sakineh Mohammadi Ashtiani, a woman recently convicted of adultery in an Iranian court and sentenced to death by stoning.

Moral outrage in a case like this is an appropriate response, but it is important to look closely at what we are responding to when we feel outrage. Is it to the method of execution or to the disproportion between the crime and the punishment, or is it to the disparity between the courts' treatment of men and women? Perhaps it is to all three; perhaps it is to something more substantial.

Some people insist that it is inappropriate to criticize the moral practices of other cultures. There is an old and popular expression that says, "When in Rome, do as the Romans do," which is often used to defend the idea that right and wrong are really just cultural conventions.

The earliest articulation of this notion occurs in *The Histories* by the Greek historian Herodotus. He recounts a story about Darius, a Persian king from the 5th century B.C. Darius was interested in learning about various cultural beliefs and practices, so he would question people from the lands bordering his kingdom.

During his reign, Darius summoned the Hellenes at his court and asked them how much money they would accept for eating the bodies of their dead fathers. They answered that they would not do that for any amount of money. Later, Darius summoned some Indians called Kallatiai, who do eat their dead parents. In the presence of the Hellenes, with an interpreter to inform them of what was said, he asked the Indians how much money they would accept to burn the bodies of their dead fathers. They responded with an outcry, ordering him to shut his mouth lest he offend the gods.

On the face of it, the Hellenes and the Kallatiai had very different moral beliefs: The Hellenes believed it was necessary to burn their dead relatives, and the Kallatiai believed it was necessary to eat them. And yet everything depends on how we describe the situation, for both the Hellenes and the Kallatiai had distinctive cultural rituals by which they expressed reverence for the dead, and ignoring those rituals, by doing something else with dead bodies, was regarded as an act of irreverence. So we could say that both the Hellenes and the Kallatiai had the same ethical views, namely, that one should always express reverence toward dead relatives. In other words, they had different rules for proper treatment of the dead, but their respective rules were based on the same ethical principle.

It is an indisputable fact that different cultures have different ethical norms or standards, but it is not possible to reduce ethics to those cultural norms. We should look carefully at cultural differences and neither immediately dismiss as ethically wrong those that are unfamiliar nor simplistically accept all practices as morally neutral.

I wonder how an Iranian apologist of the stoning of Ms. Ashtiani would respond to some of our punishments?

Teresa Lewis is on death row in Virginia (one of four states that retains the electric chair as an optional form of execution). She confessed to conspiring to kill her husband and stepson, was convicted, and sentenced to death. The two actual shooters received sentences of life in prison. Lewis has an IQ score of 72, which is considered borderline for intellectual disability. She is scheduled to be executed Sept. 23.

Executions are so common in the United States that coverage of them rarely makes it past local news, but a stoning in Iran makes headlines around the world.

How should we react to the impending stoning of Ashtiani? With moral outrage, of course, but not because our practices are somehow more civilized than Iran's. We should react with the same outrage to any serious assault on human dignity. If we feel the burn of indignation towards those who are responsible for the sentencing of Ashtiani, shouldn't we feel the same way toward those responsible in the case of Lewis?

The fact that we don't feel the same way can be explained culturally, but it cannot be justified.

August 15, 2010

NATURE

53. Thinking Like Leopold

This morning I'm sitting on the patio of a home in Colorado Springs looking west at Pikes Peak. The mountains stretching to the north and south of the Peak make up part of what is known as the "Front Range." It's a beautiful view, and the patio on which I am sitting is designed to take advantage of it.

The view is not without discomfort, however. The casual visitor to the area cannot help but notice what many of the residents seem to overlook, namely, that one of the mountains, just a little east and north of Pikes Peak, has had its top third removed, so that it presents to the viewer a large flat surface, like an upturned face, geometrically inconsonant with the neighboring peaks. An inquiry to my host reveals that a mining company holds a lease on the property, and that the mountain was strip mined to acquire a pink colored rock known as "Pikes Peak granite," used for landscaping in the region. In fact, the patio on which I am sitting is bordered by this very same rock, which may have been mined from the mountain we are viewing.

This is the sort of thing Aesop might have written a fable about: building a house to look out over the mountains but destroying the mountains to build the house.

Most of our assaults on the natural world are not as directly illogical as this, but many are close: using boats to catch fish in the Gulf, but killing the fish with the oil used to power the boats; creating a resort in the wilderness, but cutting down the forests to make room for more lodging; building a cabin on a remote northern lake, only to discover that the lake has more weekend traffic than the street at home; putting up feeders to attract birds because we've destroyed all their natural food sources with herbicides.

What kind of ethical obligation do we have towards mountains—or lakes, rivers, streams, forests, and meadows? In Aldo Leopold's famous essay, "Thinking Like a Mountain," he describes the thought that came to him while working for the U.S. Forest Service in Arizona: our efforts to shape the natural world to our liking are often done out of narrow-minded interests and an inability to appreciate the far-reaching consequences of our actions. What results is frequently counter to our own interests.

He recounts the time he shot a wolf and her cubs on the side of a mountain, a common practice at the time in the effort to increase the size of the deer herd: "I realized then, and have known ever since, that there was something new to me in those eyes— something known only to her and to the mountain....I now suspect that just as a deer herd lives in mortal fear of its wolves, so does a mountain live in mortal fear of its deer. And perhaps with better cause, for while a buck pulled down by wolves can be replaced in two or three years, a range pulled down by too many deer may fail of replacement in as many decades."

Leopold's enduring lesson for us is that the basis for living ethically in the world is to see fully—and accurately—the relationships among things. In *A Sand County Almanac* he sums it up this way: "We abuse land because we regard it as a commodity belonging to us. When we see land as a community to which we belong, we may begin to use it with love and respect."

Selective perception comes easily to most of us. We tend to see what we want to see and not to see the things that are inconvenient. What really requires effort is unselective perception—seeing what is actually there to see. It's hard because it may force us to change the way we live. But that's what we do when we love someone—or something. We adapt ourselves to preserve the relationship, and ultimately our lives are richer because of it.

August 1, 2010

54. Hunting

Robert Marshall, co-founder of the Wilderness Society, predicted that wild places would acquire even more value as they became scarce. He thought, as many did in the early 20th century, that wilderness is an ineluctable human need, like food, water, and security, and that the less people have, the more they will desire it.

But history has proven him wrong. Wilderness appears instead to be an evanescent good, like art or literature. The less we have, the less it is desired. In its absence, other things, arguably less valuable, take its place. (Facebook, anyone?)

In his best-selling book, *Last Child in the Woods*, Richard Louv documents how our society is raising a generation of children who are technologically adept but ecologically illiterate. He refers to the condition as "nature-deficit disorder," a condition characterized by both indifference to and fear of the outdoors.

My own introduction to and, ultimately, infatuation with wild places came through hunting and fishing, but by the time I had children of my own, I had effectively given them up as serious pursuits. We were living in a big city, and instead of going hunting and fishing, we would read our kids nature books, take them to the zoo, go on trail hikes, and the occasional camping trip. All of which are fine entertainments. But they allow children merely to observe—not to have a participatory relationship with—wild things.

So I began hunting and fishing again with regularity, making those activities part of a seasonal routine integral to my life, so that I could introduce our children to the natural world in the same manner that I was introduced to it, and my father before me, and his father before him.

Ever since then I have been challenged to defend that choice to non-hunters. Here is that defense—at least an abbreviated version of it.

Without hunters and anglers, there would be far fewer ducks, geese, elk, deer, turkeys, and trout than there are today, not to mention songbirds, butterflies, and a host of other non-game species.

The most effective conservation organizations in the country are comprised primarily of hunters and anglers. Organizations like Ducks Unlimited, Delta Waterfowl, Trout Unlimited, the Wild Turkey Federation, the Ruffed Grouse Society, Pheasants Forever, and so on, have restored millions of acres of precious habitat for game and non-game species. The Pittman-Robertson Wildlife Restoration Act, an excise tax on hunting firearms and ammunition dating from 1937, provides most of the funding for wildlife habitat acquisition and rehabilitation overseen by state fish and wildlife departments.

In this country, we kill far more wild animals through pollution, land development, traffic, and invasive species, than by hunting, trapping, and fishing. When you also consider the number of domestic animals killed in factory farms for the food industry, the numbers aren't even close. The person who commutes to work thirty miles a day kills more wildlife than the average hunter, and the person who flushes his prescription medications down the toilet kills more fish than the typical weekend angler.

Aldo Leopold observed in *A Sand County Almanac* that not owning a farm creates two spiritual dangers: "One is the danger of supposing that breakfast comes from the grocery, and the other that heat comes from the furnace." The same can be said for not hunting. Hunting encourages a frank acknowledgment of the tragic cost of living in the world.

The effect that killing an animal for food has on the hunter is the realization that living in the world has irreversible consequences for others. Animals die so we may live. We may hide those consequences by means of technology and industrialization, but they exist nevertheless.

The wood ducks my son and I killed last weekend were beautiful and nourishing. Just as beautiful, I imagine, as the many millions of wild creatures destroyed by the encroaching omnipresence of the human species across the earth. But these particular ducks were killed by our own hands, and that's a fact we cannot hide from ourselves. It somehow makes the remaining wildness seem more intimately tied to who we are and how we go about our daily lives, and therefore more precious.

October 10, 2010

55. Contemplation

Five people asked me this past week if I was going turkey hunting. I'm not. I never have. For two reasons: I don't have a place to do it, and I don't like turkeys. In fact, I despise them.

I grew up in Frazee, Minnesota, home of the "world's largest turkey," the annual Turkey Days parade, and the Miss Turkey pageant. My grandfather was a turkey farmer. My earliest memory is of standing in a turkey pen, looking up at their ugly bald heads, detecting malicious intent in their beady black eyes, bewildered by their wattles. I have had quite enough of turkeys, thank you very much.

But besides all that, I simply don't need another addictive outdoor activity to compete with the others that already engage my time and attention. What turkey hunters find in the woods, I already find along the trout stream, on the deer stand, and in the duck blind. That is, the opportunity for contemplation.

In talking to turkey hunters, the two things that occur over and over in their accounts is the delight they take in watching the world come alive in the early morning and the anticipation of a turkey that can be heard gobbling just out of sight, and is often never seen.

The turkey hunter can confirm, better perhaps than anyone else, the truth of Thoreau's words: "You only need sit still long enough in some attractive spot in the woods that all its inhabitants may exhibit themselves to you by turns."

I don't know why it is that I can't get myself out of bed at 4 a.m. just to go out and sit quietly in the woods. However, if I'm going hunting or fishing, I have a hard time sleeping at all and usually wake up before the alarm. Maybe it's a lack of discipline, but I'm not alone in this peculiar failing. Nobody I know regularly goes out into the woods before sunrise just to sit and watch and listen.

Practically all the most memorable moments I have had hunting and fishing were incidental: a great horned owl swooping down on my head as I settled into a predawn duck blind; a family of beavers wrestling and diving and coming back up to wrestle again on an ice shelf in a secluded northern pond; brook trout leaping out of the water to snatch mayflies from the air on the first warm day of spring.

I know the discrepancy between what I seek and what I value, but it's hard to put into words. When I tell someone I've been fishing, the first question is: "How many did you catch?" I caught hundreds of trout last year, but the coolest thing I caught was sight of a doe and fawn playing tag in a stream, running, splashing, slipping and sliding on the wet rocks until they came within a rod's length. That experience is not what I went out to get, but it was the most valuable thing I came away with all season, measured by the number of times I've thought about it since.

Perhaps the greatest indictment of contemporary culture is that we have lost the language for expressing the value of non-utilitarian activity. If we cannot demonstrate how it helps the bottom line, how it puts food on the table, or a roof over our heads, it's hard to justify. And yet, a sizeable percentage of our national economy is dedicated to spectator sports and entertainment.

Some activities, such as watching television, playing cards, or shopping are simply pastimes; they are ways of losing time in idleness. But other activities, like painting, writing, gardening, praying, birding, hunting, and fishing, require attentive waiting. They are exercises in contemplation.

The value of such activities is not in what they produce, but in what happens to us as we participate in them. We become more reverent, more observant, more aware that all of life is like this: long stretches of waiting punctuated by brief moments of significance that, if we are asleep, or distracted, or daydreaming, we miss altogether.

If only it didn't involve turkeys, I think I might take up turkey hunting. For the good of my soul.

April 22, 2012

56. WILDERNESS

Why should we preserve wild places?

The answer generally given by those most involved in the conservationist movement is that we owe it to future generations. This answer is repeated in defense of setting aside fragile ecosystems, designating roadless areas, granting conservation easements, protecting the river bluffs, and establishing stricter zoning codes in counties.

But defending conservation practices in this way is problematic. It presupposes that developing policies for wise land use is a contest between the preferences of future generations and the needs of the present. It raises the question of why the interests of certain groups of people, such as hunters, anglers, trappers, hikers, and birdwatchers, should have precedence over the interests of home owners, automobile drivers, golfers, and bottled water consumers.

In fact, the debate in this country over land use has become emblematic of American democracy: a struggle between competing special interest groups to influence common laws and policies through elections.

But this is not the only way to frame the debate.

In *Reflections from the North Country,* Sigurd Olson, the conservationist and author principally responsible for the preservation of the Boundary Waters Canoe Area Wilderness, takes up the question of why we should care about wild places. He cites people like Paul Sears: "Conservation is a point of view involved with the whole concept of freedom, dignity, and the American spirit."

And this from Harvey Broome, one the founders of the Wilderness Society: "Without wilderness, we will eventually lose the capacity to understand America.... If we lose wilderness, we lose forever the knowledge of what the world was and what it might, with understanding and loving husbandry, yet become."

For Olson, like many of his contemporaries, the outdoors wasn't just a place for recreation; it was essential to the development of moral character. And therefore the defense of conservation was not a defense of the special interests of a certain group of Americans; it was a defense of America itself.

That is why Sterling North could say, "Every time you see a dust cloud, a muddy stream, a field scarred by erosions, or a channel choked with silt, you are witnessing the passing of American democracy."

Preserving open spaces, ensuring clean air and water, protecting wildlife and maintaining the diversity of species for the benefit of future generations was, to be sure, important to the early conservationists.

But they also regarded shortsighted development and exploitation of resources to be self-destructive and foolish, a sign not only of disregard for our children and grand-children, but a symptom of disorder in our present lives. They worried that if such disorder became pervasive in society, it could destroy American culture, leading to a nation characterized by pettiness, greed, and incivility.

Even a brief time spent in a natural setting allows one to experience the vital importance of things that can be appreciated but not possessed. It provides for the realization of an order of value that is not created or manipulated by society, but is eternally present. Without such experiences, life becomes a contest limited by the economy of the marketplace, of buying, selling, and trading—none of which are bad things, unless they are mistaken for the goal rather than the means.

Without natural places, we have no way of getting outside of the humanly constructed environment to gain perspective on our lives.

Olson himself put it best: "The conservation of waters, forests, mountains, and wildlife is far more than saving terrain. It is the conservation of the human spirit which is the goal."

That's a goal worthy of America's best effort.

July 31, 2011

57. Places

Earnest Hemingway's "Now I Lay Me" tells the story of Nick Adams, a wounded soldier lying in a hospital bed in France, afraid that if he falls asleep he will never wake up again. To stay awake he imagines himself back home in Michigan fishing his favorite trout stream. He recreates the place in his imagination down to the last detail, and he fishes the stream, from beginning to end, every night.

When I first read that story years ago, I didn't appreciate its power. I had not yet discovered that there are a few special places where one feels fully alive, and there are times when one must draw upon the memory of those places to sustain one's life.

Those places are, of course, different for everyone, but for myself, as for Nick Adams, they happen to be wild places, and living a life without the memory of those places is nearly unimaginable.

The waterfowl season opens this weekend in Wisconsin and Minnesota. For older hunters like me, the best part of duck hunting is generally the hour before sunrise: the decoys are in place, the blind is set up, and there is nothing to do but wait and listen and remember. No matter where I am, the smell of wet dog, the taste of stale coffee, and the sound of wing beats overhead take me back to Gray's Lake where I learned to hunt 40 years ago.

The fact that people of my generation have places like that to remember, and that our children today are forming sustaining memories of their own in such places, should not be taken for granted. In the 1930s waterfowl populations were at an all-time low. Farmers had filled in wetlands and drought had dried up the prairie pot holes in the duck breeding regions of the Dakotas and Saskatchewan.

But over the past few decades waterfowl populations have rebounded, with some species reaching record levels. The story of how that occurred is complicated, but it is important to note, especially since ducks numbers are once again being threatened by drought and changing land use.

A significant part of that story is Ducks Unlimited, formed in 1937 by a small group of sportsmen dedicated to conserving waterfowl habitat. The organization has since become the largest private conservation organization in the world with nearly 600,000 members who have conserved or influenced over 100,000,000 acres of waterfowl habitat in North America.

Another part of the story is the Federal Aid in Wildlife Restoration Act (known as the "Pittman-Robertson Act"). Signed into law in 1937, this federal tax is collected from the purchase of firearms and hunting equipment and used to fund habitat improvement, hunter education, wildlife research, and to acquire public hunting lands.

The Conservation Reserve Program, which provides payments to farmers to convert marginally productive land into wildlife habitat, has been crucial to restoring waterfowl breeding grounds. Thirty-two million acres are currently enrolled in CRP, mostly in the Prairie Pothole Region, but the program could be greatly reduced in the next version of the Farm Bill.

It is easy to overlook the many ways our personal lives are intertwined with complex, bureaucratic matters like non-profit organizations, taxes, state and federal policies, government agencies, and research. But all one has to do is connect the dots to see that nearly everything one considers important, even those rare experiences that make up the very substance of one's identity, are dependent upon the decisions of people one has never met and will never know.

I wonder what would have happened to Nick Adams if he did not have trout streams to fish in his youth. What memories would have sustained him then? What places in our children's lives today have the capacity to enrich their souls and sustain them through difficult times?

This weekend I will be hunting with my son on the backwaters of the Upper Mississippi River Refuge. While my attention is diverted by fond memories of hunting with my dad on Gray's Lake, he will be fully present, forming his own memories of a place and time that may one day have the power to sustain him.

This is just my way of saying "thank you" to the people who made that possible.

September 23, 2012

58. Dogs

"If you're gonna train a dog," my grandpa used to say, "you've gotta be smarter than the dog." That's easier said than done.

Mickey, our American Water Spaniel, was five months old, and we had just come home from hunting ducks. He was covered in muck from snout to tail and smelled like the Mississippi River bottoms.

"That dog needs a bath right now," Cindi said as we stepped into the porch. "Okay," I said, "just as soon as I take off my boots." When I turned around, Mickey was nowhere to be seen. I looked all over the house, hoping not to find him curled up on a bed or sofa, but he wasn't in any of the places I feared.

Finally I checked the bathroom, and there he was: standing in the tub, shaking in dread anticipation of the bath, an ordeal he hated more than anything.

How had he known what to do? We had only given him a bath in the tub one time, and we had not taught him any bath-taking commands. Had he caught just the one word, "bath," and taken it as an order, or was he in the habit of listening to our conversations, trying to anticipate what we wanted him to do?

Invite a room full of people to share stories of dogs doing surprising things and you'll open up a conversation topic that could go on for hours. Such stories reveal how grossly we underestimate their intelligence.

Like the story my dad tells about a dog on their farm who liked to join in games of "hide-and-seek," taking his turn as "hider" and "seeker" just like all the other kids. Nobody trained him to play the game; he most likely learned because the kids were too young to "know" that dogs could only follow simple commands.

One of the best books I've read in recent years is *Merle's Door,* by Ted Kerasote. It is the story of a man learning how to live with an adopted dog, and in the process coming to acknowledge the richness of animal intelligence, character, and emotion—attributes which philosophers and psychologists have long denied.

One-hundred years of behavioral psychology has convinced many that to attribute character traits to animals is to be guilty of "anthropomorphism," mistakenly thinking that animals can feel and reason just like people. But those who spend a great deal of time working with animals find it impossible to accurately describe dogs (or horses or dolphins or elephants) without speaking of the virtues and vices—like courage, generosity, perseverance, and spitefulness—that make each of them an individual with its own personality, sometimes endearing, sometimes frustrating.

The ethical challenge posed by animals is the same as that posed by people who are different from us in some significant way—the constant temptation to treat them merely as things (instruments, commodities, obstacles) and not as beings with intrinsic worth.

What we owe all animals is to treat them with the respect they deserve. The terms of that respect, however, differ with each species and can be discovered only by living in proximity with them and paying attention to their needs, abilities, and characteristics.

In the case of dogs, that means, among other things, giving them something important to do, some role in the household economy, like taking their owners for a walk, or keeping the castle safe from intruders, or flushing grouse. (I have no idea what the terms of respect are for cats, except that it has something to do with allowing them their privacy.)

I can sometimes force my dog to do what I want him to

do, but I cannot force him to be the kind of companion I want him to be. For that to happen, I have to humble myself, and become worthy of him, by granting him a meaningful place in my life—neither coddling nor abusing him.

To treat my dog with respect I have to learn to treat him neither as a person nor as a thing, but as a dog. To do that I have to unlearn the simplistic notions of animal intelligence prevalent in our society and instead concentrate on working out and then abiding by the expectations we have of one another. Doing that successfully is a daily test of character, for both of us.

November 4, 2012

59. ANIMALS

Last night we had a mouse in the house.

It ran across the kitchen floor, into the back porch, and disappeared.

We live in an old house, and despite my best efforts to seal cracks in the foundation, every fall one or two mice manage to find their way into this sanctuary of warmth and cereal crumbs. Usually our cat catches them, but sometimes I have to do it.

Which raises the question: is there an ethical way to dispatch a mouse?

Worrying about the most ethical way to rid one's house of rodents may seem trifling, but our daily, trivial ethical challenges are inextricably linked to bigger, more substantial issues. The questions raised by our response to a mouse in the house are the same as those raised by hogs in factory farms or chickens in pens. Does the suffering of animals matter? Are we responsible for that suffering? What should we do about it?

Animal rights organizations such as People for the Ethical Treatment of Animals (PETA) and The Humane Society of the United States (HSUS) oppose the use of traps that kill rodents in favor of more humane methods of control.

Their argument—not only about mice but about all animals—is based on a type of moral reasoning known as utilitarianism. In its most basic form, it goes like this:

We should do what we can to increase pleasure and decrease pain in the world.

Activities such as trapping, shooting, experimenting, caging, and so on, cause avoidable suffering to animals.

Therefore, those activities are unethical.

The argument is simple and powerful.

Those who disagree point out that animals are not people,

so we do not have the same kinds of moral obligations to them as we do toward one another.

But one of the principal theorists for the animal rights movement, Peter Singer, calls that attitude "speciesism." He writes, "the fact that beings are not members of our species does not entitle us to exploit them, and similarly the fact that other animals are less intelligent than we are does not mean that their interests may be disregarded."

He is surely right about that. Animals may not have the same rights as people, but the fact that they can experience pleasure and pain is morally significant, and we should take responsibility for the suffering we cause them.

Most people, I suspect, agree with this. Much animal suffering takes place, not because people don't think it matters, but because they do not witness it.

And yet, I am not convinced that the utilitarian argument for animal rights is sound. The suffering of animals matters, but it is not the only thing that matters.

In my previous column, I argued that we have an obligation to treat both people and animals with respect—as possessors of intrinsic worth, not merely as things. This means that animals should not be regarded as mere commodities, but it also implies that the meaning of their lives is not limited to their capacity for pleasure and pain.

My favorite photo of Aldo Leopold shows him sitting in the grass. A hunting vest lies discarded upon a folding chair behind him; a shotgun can be seen upon the hood of a car in the background. In his hand he holds a dead woodcock, about to weigh it on a scale.

Leopold did not hunt woodcock because he was insensitive to their suffering; rather he did it in acknowledgement of the many ways that human beings are already bound up in the life and death of other species.

The photo reminds me of the grave responsibility we have toward animals, creatures who are dependent upon us to a far greater extent than we realize. We have not only direct power over them as individual beings, but also the power to affect, for good or ill, their species, by preserving, destroying, or otherwise altering the basic conditions of collective existence.

A mouse in the house may seem trivial, but how we deal with the mouse is not. Animals—whether mice, deer, turkeys, or woodcock—matter, and the question of how we treat them is among the most significant questions we will ever face.

November 18, 2012

60. REGULATION

A rich vein of taconite runs through the Penokee Hills in northern Wisconsin. Twenty-two miles long, 1.5 miles wide, and 1500 feet deep, the resource contains an estimated 20% of our nation's remaining iron ore deposits. Gogebic Taconite, a subsidiary of the Cline Group (a West Virginia coal mining company) wants to put a strip mine there.

Residents of Ashland and Iron counties are wary. They are concerned about the effects a large-scale mining operation would have on the Bad River watershed.

According to Frank Koehn, president of the Penokee Hills Education Project, legislation is being drafted this fall that would revise Wisconsin's current mining regulations. Reports of the draft bill suggest that the new law would fast-track the approval process, curtail opportunities for public input, exempt the mining companies from local zoning ordinances, and allow dumping of wastes into the watershed.

All mines have negative effects on someone, but some mines have more negative effects than others. It is through the painstaking process of regulation that the details of who pays the costs get worked out. Some of the costs are easy to determine and immediate, some are long-term and harder to estimate.

Iron ore processing requires approximately 1300 gallons of water per ton of taconite; Gogebic estimates that they will produce 8 million tons of taconite per year. That means 10,400,000,000 gallons of water will be taken out of the watershed yearly.

The Bad River watershed includes numerous brook trout streams, sturgeon spawning areas, and the largest wild rice bed in North America. What is that watershed worth? Who pays for it if it gets destroyed?

In his memoir *The Land Remembers,* Ben Logan writes about the drought that afflicted Wisconsin farms in the 1930s.

> From the drying up of the wells we learned that the need to protect the land was not just local. A state geologist explained what he thought had happened. Much of the well water in southwestern Wisconsin came from a layer of limestone buried three-hundred feet or more below the surface of the ridges. That layer of limestone slanted upward, to the north, so that a hundred miles away, in north central Wisconsin, the limestone lay at the surface. There, it picked up water. That water seeped slowly southward through the limestone to our wells, taking perhaps seventy-five years to make the trip. And about seventy-five years before, the geologist pointed out, men had drained the surface water from the north central Wisconsin marshes to make more farmland.
>
> The story of the seventy-five-year-old well water and the draining of the marshes made a deep impression on Father. "There's just too much we don't know," he said. "How could somebody way up there know he was draining away our water supply? For that matter what are we doing right here that's changing things someplace else?
>
> "I guess we can't be expected to know everything in advance," Mother said gently.
>
> "That's right. But we can damn well go slow when we start changing things. We can admit that we're playing around with something that's a lot bigger than we are."

Wisconsin has the strictest mining regulations in the U.S. The Cline Group would prefer the state's regulations to be similar to those of other states, where the permitting process is friendlier to mining interests.

But the current laws are there for good reason. They ensure significant economic benefit to the residents of the state and protection for sensitive environmental areas. They also require opportunities for public input. In short, they ensure that the burden of paying for the costs falls upon those who reap the benefits.

Sometimes government does a poor job of regulation. It can be slow, burdensome, overly complicated, and inconsistent. But regulation is a necessity. Mining companies have little incentive to pay attention to long-term consequences, so the incentives need to be mandated.

The purpose of government regulation is to protect the common good—to ensure the integrity of those things that we cannot possess individually but must share in common if we are to have them at all—things like clean air and water, healthy food, and safety.

When it comes to the common good, you can't fast-track doing the right thing.

September 25, 2011

61. Leopold's Legacy

What is land worth?

With increasing demand for steel in China and India, low-grade iron ore deposits like the Penokee Hills have become potentially profitable. One estimate puts the value of taconite in those hills at around $200 billion.

Mining companies are paying three to five times the market value to obtain land for frac-sand operations in western Wisconsin.

Such facts imply a simple answer to the question of what land is worth: "whatever someone is willing to pay for it."

But simple answers can be misleading, evident as soon as one asks what honor, freedom, friendship, or life is worth.

We regard some things as having inestimable value, which is not to say we don't make economic calculations regarding them. Insurance companies estimate what a person will pay for health care. We don't assume that amount to reflect the value of a person's life.

Yet, we commonly make a mistake with land, assuming that purchase price reflects sum total value, and that ownership confers rights with few corresponding obligations.

In 1933 the farms in Coon Valley had lost much of their worth. Overgrazing and poor erosion control had nearly destroyed the land. Even moderate rainfalls washed out roads, gullies became too large to cross, and the streams were choked with sediment. The condition of the land was so compromised and the farmers so desperate that the newly formed Soil Conservation Service selected it as the site of the nation's first watershed restoration project.

The land owners in Coon Valley were persuaded that accepting help with new practices like strip cropping, terracing, and stream bank stabilization would save their farms. And it did. Within a few years the slopes were retaining topsoil, the streams were running clear, and the crops were improving.

Aldo Leopold, who was at the time a professor of game management at the University of Wisconsin–Madison served as extension advisor and documented the project in his essay, "Coon Valley: An Adventure in Cooperative Conservation."

Now, eighty years later, people from all over the world know about Coon Valley. They read about it in books, study it in courses, and some even make the pilgrimage to its picturesque landscape. But many who live within an hour's drive have little notion of its history or significance.

The Coon Valley watershed restoration project succeeded, and continues to inspire people today, because it demonstrated that human beings do not have to destroy the land to benefit from it and that land restoration can provide a recipe for restoring the human spirit. Leopold expressed it simply: "land health and human good are inseparable." Whatever we do to the land we do to ourselves.

Today, as the citizens of Wisconsin deliberate the terms of iron-ore mining, frac-sand mining, water quality, wetlands abatement, high capacity wells, corn ethanol production, and large scale dairy farms, it is important to keep the lessons of Coon Valley in mind. Land is not a disposable resource. It is misused and discarded only at great cost, the extent of which cannot be measured by the market alone.

What is missing from many of our public debates is a commitment to what Leopold called a "harmonious, balanced system of land use," a commitment that stems from acknowledging our mutual dependence on the land not only for a healthy economy but for a flourishing, robust, fully human life.

Next Saturday people in communities throughout Wisconsin will gather to celebrate Aldo Leopold Weekend, to read aloud from *A Sand County Almanac* and also, most importantly, talk about the present day significance of his ideas. Because, as Leopold himself said, "nothing so important as an ethic is ever 'written'.... It evolves in the mind of a thinking community."

And nothing devalues land so quickly as a community that stops thinking about the fundamental conditions for sustaining human life.

February 24, 2013

62. STEWARDSHIP

In March 1940, Aldo Leopold gave an address to the Fifth North American Wildlife Conference. He concluded his remarks with this sentence: "To change ideas about what land is for is to change ideas about what anything is for."

Leopold was speaking at a time when leaders of the wilderness movement were expressing concerns about the loss of wilderness and its adverse effect on American culture. Robert Marshall, one of the cofounders of the Wilderness Society, remarked: "As society becomes more and more mechanized, it will be more and more difficult for many people to stand the nervous strain, the high pressure, and the drabness of their lives. To escape these abominations, constantly growing numbers will seek the primitive for the fine features of life."

Marshall, like many of his contemporaries, took a utilitarian, or cost-benefit, approach. He argued that the value of wilderness will increase proportionally as wilderness becomes scarcer. As people lose opportunities for relaxation and contemplation, they will seek even harder to find and will be willing to pay more for those opportunities.

Leopold's voice was distinctive from his contemporaries in that he rejected the utilitarian approach outright. Indeed, he went so far as to say, "I doubt if there exists today a more complete regimentation of the human mind than that accomplished by our self-imposed doctrine of ruthless utilitarianism."

We can see the effects of "ruthless utilitarianism" today in the Wisconsin legislature's proposal to drastically cut Stewardship funding. The proposal betrays two assumptions:

1. Public land is not economically productive.
2. Only economic production matters.

Marshall would dispute the first assumption; Leopold would dispute the second.

Public land is not economically productive in a direct sense, but if used wisely can generate many times its value for private business. A survey by the National Association of Home Realtors, for example, discovered that the second most important community amenity for prospective home buyers is access to trails. Another example is the economic impact of outdoor activities such as trout fishing, which, according to a recent study by Northstar Economics, amounts to $1.1 billion per year in the Driftless region alone.

Where does public access to trails and streams come from? In Wisconsin, it comes mostly from the Stewardship Program.

The Knowles-Nelson Stewardship Program was established in 1989 to preserve land through purchase and easements, to restore wildlife habitat, and to promote outdoor recreation. Over 500,000 acres have been protected through the program. During the last budget cycle the legislature cut funding from $86 million to $60 million per year. This time around the Joint Finance Committee has proposed cutting the allocation an additional $12.5 million for 2013–14 while also selling off 10,000 acres of previously acquired property.

It is difficult to say just how much land the state should conserve, because it is not a simple question of amount. There are also questions of how to conserve land (through purchase or easement), where to conserve it (in rural or urban areas), and for what purpose (for hunting and fishing, logging, hiking, or ATV use). But such questions, though difficult and at times contentious, are answerable.

Robert Marshall's advice was not to take a short-sighted view of things. As the population increases, and undeveloped land becomes scarcer, the value of the remaining land will increase. As other, more populous states continue to squander their natural resources, states that take measures to protect natural areas will reap the long-term economic benefits.

Aldo Leopold was not satisfied with that reasoning. His resistance to framing questions about the value of land in terms of economic costs and benefits was that it skewed our perception, not just of land but of everything we care about.

In the foreword to *A Sand County Almanac*, Leopold writes: "That land is a community is the basic concept of ecology, but that land is to be loved and respected is an extension of ethics. That land yields a cultural harvest is a fact long known, but latterly often forgotten."

The question raised by the debate over funding the Stewardship Program is not simply one of economic foresight. It is also, and more significantly, a question of cultural foresight. Who are we, and who do we wish to become? The answer will be determined in large part by what we do with the land entrusted to us.

June 2, 2013

63. SAND

Van Potter tells the story of standing in a Wisconsin marsh with Aldo Leopold, watching a flock of Sandhill Cranes fly overhead. He remarked on their beauty; Leopold replied, "Now, make sure you learn more about what you love."

Merely loving something does not ensure its protection. This is abundantly clear when it comes to the Driftless region ecosystem and the recent debates over frac-sand mining.

For the past decade I've been trying to learn more about the spring creeks that flow through the valleys of the Driftless region. But it's a difficult task. There is so much information available, and my ability to comprehend it so limited, that I feel inadequate to the task.

There are approximately 7,000 miles of cold water streams in the Driftless region; nearly all of them are fed by springs, thus the name "spring creeks." La Crosse County has 28 spring creeks stretching 109 miles. Vernon County has 68 creeks stretching 299 miles. Monroe County has 80 creeks stretching 260 miles. Just those three counties alone add up to 668 miles of spring creeks.

Even people who have lived in this region their entire lives don't realize how extremely rare these spring creeks are. According to Ted Leeson's *Jerusalem Creek,* of the world's surface water, only 1 millionth of it (.0001%) flows in rivers or streams. Of all the water in the world's rivers and streams, only about one millionth of 1% flows in cold water streams. Of those cold water streams, only about one-thousandth of the water flows in spring creeks.

These creeks constitute the arteries of an incredibly rich and diverse ecosystem. One biologist I spoke with estimated that approximately 80% of native Wisconsin species inhabit the Driftless region.

These creeks are not only a natural resource, they are a significant economic resource as well. In 2008, Northstar Economics conducted an assessment of the economic impact of trout fishing in the Driftless region. They found that trout angling contributes $1.1 billion annually to the Driftless region economy. Of course, much of that goes unnoticed. Trout anglers don't all fish together on the same streams, stay at the same hotels, and eat at the same restaurants. They seek secluded places, so it's easy to overlook their presence and thus their economic contribution.

Frac-sand mines are not easy to overlook. They are large, unsightly, and multiplying at a rate no one could have predicted just a few years ago. Since the entire region is rich in the small uniformly sized silica sand granules used in the hydraulic fracturing process that is transforming natural gas extraction, many more mines are on the way. No one seems to know how many to expect.

A few sand mines probably won't have much effect, but hundreds of them could drastically change the landscape. Will that change be good for us, or will it destroy what we love about this region? Will it deter tourists from coming here? Will it make it harder to attract other businesses and employees to the region?

The answers to such questions depend in large part upon what happens to the land once the mining is over. Companies like Applied Ecological Services have demonstrated the ability to restore lands damaged by mining, landfills, and toxic wastes. But the process takes planning. Counties and municipalities must have practical and detailed land-reclamation requirements in place before the mining starts.

With wise leadership from local government, appreciating what we already have, understanding the present situation, and putting in place protections for the future, this region should be able to enjoy economic vitality without sacrificing quality of life. Poor leadership will result in a landscape pock-marked by open sores, a fragile ecosystem facing collapse, and the prospect of long-term economic health in ruins.

In another conversation between Ben Logan and Aldo Leopold, the latter observed, "You can't pick up anything one at a time. It's all fastened together."

Wise policies should always begin with that fact in mind.

March 25, 2012

64. WATER

The Ogallala Aquifer is drying up.

North America's largest underground source of fresh water, it stretches from South Dakota to Texas and covers portions of eight western states. In parts of Kansas and Texas the water level has dropped more than 150 feet.

Some towns in the Texas panhandle have no drinking water, and farmers are going bankrupt due to lack of irrigation. Hoping to avoid a similar fate, residents of northwest Kansas recently agreed to a voluntary 20% reduction in water usage.

Kansas Governor Sam Brownback said, "If we extend the life of the aquifer, future generations will call us wise. If we don't, they'll consider us selfish. It's on us."

In a year when the Mississippi River has been running near flood stage all spring and local farmers have had difficulty planting crops due to rain, it is hard to imagine that some places in the U.S. are experiencing severe water shortage.

Groundwater does not have the variability of surface water. It can take centuries for groundwater to seep through soil and rock into aquifers, but aquifers don't lose their capacity during times of drought. That will make them even more valuable in the future, as we look to the more extreme conditions coming with a changing climate.

Aquifers only dry up when the rate of discharge exceeds the rate of recharge. Over the last fifty years, with the development of high capacity wells and sophisticated irrigation systems, water has been pumped out much faster than it can seep back in. Hydrologists estimate that it could take thousands of years to replenish the Ogallala.

Wisconsin has long been exempt from the water quantity concerns of western states.

But as the water resource runs dry in the plains, many large feed-lot and dairy operations are moving to the upper Midwest. Add to that the increased water demand from sand and mineral mining, and Wisconsin for the first time in its history is facing the possibility of being water poor.

How could that happen? Because the Department of Natural Resources does not consider the cumulative effects of water withdrawal when permitting high-capacity wells; it only looks at the immediate effects of each well considered in isolation.

It is like saying that one teaspoon of water will not affect the water level in a bathtub, so if 10,000 teaspoons of water are removed, that won't affect the water level either.

Lakes throughout the Central Sands region have historic low water levels. Homeowners on Long Lake in Waushara County (which contains 580 high-capacity wells) have docks that don't reach the shoreline. The Little Plover River, portions of which have dried up nearly every summer since 2006, was recently listed as one of the most endangered rivers in the United States.

Last week, the Joint Finance Committee of the Wisconsin State Legislature added a measure to the budget bill to prohibit the DNR from considering the cumulative effects of high capacity wells in future permitting decisions.

Water is a commons resource, a resource to which everyone has access and which everyone needs. Commons resources may be overexploited in the absence of clearly defined guidelines for multiple users. In Wisconsin, this principle is embedded in the constitution under the Public Trust Doctrine, which holds that the navigable waters of the state are held in trust by the state for all its citizens.

A commons resource requires a commons discourse. A few individuals or corporations should not be able to determine policy on a matter that intimately affects the well-being of everyone in the state, at least not without a full public discussion of the potential costs and benefits.

Just a few years ago, the residents of western Kansas thought their underground water supply was inexhaustible. Now they are learning just how much their economy and quality of life depends on decisions made by the previous generation.

To avoid the mistakes of our neighbors to the west, Wisconsin must develop long-term water use and conservation policies that are fair and beneficial to all and which protect, sustain, and renew our waters for the future. That cannot happen if water policy decisions are made through the state budget process, where long-term thinking gets short shrift.

The late Luna Leopold, son of Aldo Leopold and one of the nation's foremost hydrologists, claimed that "Water is the most critical resource issue of our lifetime and our children's lifetime."

Take a good look at what has been happening in the western states and what is beginning to happen in Wisconsin, and you will see that he was right.

June 16, 2013

SOCIETY

65. Moral Degeneration

My grandfather Emmett was a great complainer. He was a justice of the peace in Frazee, Minnesota, and that gave him a platform for expressing his many discontents.

His favorite complaint was the moral degeneration of society, and he had a long list of examples: hippies, rock music, drug use, disrespect of elders, littering, graffiti, women driving pickup trucks, television shows (except for "Bonanza" and "Hee Haw"), politicians (except for Hubert H. Humphrey) and movie stars (except for John Wayne).

Curious to know what things were like before my generation had led to society's downfall, I asked him what it was like when he was growing up. And then I would hear stories of his early adventures: tipping outhouses on Halloween, stealing watermelons, taking apart a neighbor's wagon and reassembling it on top of his barn, hustling pool, carving plug nickels. The stories went on and on. One of his favorites was about how he and other kids in his North Dakota town would approach an old man who had been a soldier in the Confederate army. They would stand in the street and sing "Marching through Georgia," taunting him until he grabbed his cane to chase them down the street. "He'd get so angry he couldn't even speak," Emmett would say. Then, after a reflective pause, "Oh, we were a terrible bunch of kids."

We find worries about the moral character of the succeeding generation expressed in all cultures at all times in history. We find them in Plato's Dialogues from 350 B.C.; we find them in the writings of Sallust and Livy during the height of the Roman Empire; we find them in newspapers from Victorian England and in early American diaries.

Centuries and centuries of people documenting the moral

degeneration of their age, and rarely do we find observations of moral improvement. Is it more likely that moral improvement rarely happens or that the observers are biased?

It is easy to find evidence that certain things in our society are getting worse, because society is large and complex. There is always someone ready to point out the latest survey showing that dishonesty in the workplace is increasing or that the high school graduation rate has reached an alarming new low.

In response, one could point out that some aspects of our society are getting better. One could point to the increasing number of young people volunteering in their communities, or the rising percentage of college students majoring in service-oriented professions.

But pointing out positive stories is only a half-measure: the tendency to complain is not due to a lack of information but to a desire to be relevant.

Finding fault with the next generation is universal because aging is universal. As we age, we discover that the universe that seemed to revolve around us in our youth is following an orbit that we don't control. So we create myths, with ourselves as the Ptolemaic center around which we draw increasingly elaborate orbits. Some of these myths, like the myth of moral degeneration, are as old as history. Others are new, like the myth of generational differences in the workplace.

But sometimes in our reflective moments these pretensions fall away and, face to face with one another, we tell our stories, in which the fears, anxieties, hopes, and joys of the parents' youth are seen through the eyes of the children. The stories are what bring us together. They give witness to the tie that binds, a common humanity the years do not erode.

March 7, 2010

66. BULLYING

Is bullying on the rise?

It certainly seems to be. Journalists are writing more stories about it. Documentary filmmakers are producing features about it. School boards and administrators are writing new policies to address it. Parents are more concerned about it.

The National Center for Education Studies reported that bullying at schools increased 25% from 2003 to 2007. A Massachusetts study found a 50% increase in reported bullying from 1983 to 2003. An estimated 160,000 children stay home from school each day for fear of being bullied.

The 2008 National Survey of Children's Exposure to Violence, a comprehensive study sponsored by the Department of Justice and the Centers for Disease Control, found that over 60% of American children had been exposed to violence within the previous year.

The numbers certainly seem alarming. But it is hard to know whether the national statistics indicate that bullying is increasing or whether students are simply more willing to report it.

One of the problems with emphasizing the increase in bullying is that it may have the effect of encouraging even more bullying by making it seem more prevalent than it actually is. Sociologists have long warned about a phenomenon known as "misperception of norms," in which the false belief that a certain behavior is normal will tend to increase the behavior. For instance, college students who believe that a majority of other students drink alcohol regularly are likely to drink more often themselves.

What this means is that simply drawing attention to bullying may not be the best way to prevent it. It is just as likely to cause kids to regard bullying behavior as normal and inevitable.

But just as it is possible to increase bullying by making it seem normal, it may be possible to reduce or even eliminate bullying by making it appear unacceptable.

Skeptics, of course, insist that it is impossible to eliminate bullying. They say it is human nature for some kids to tease other kids; it is just part of growing up. You might be able to reduce it somewhat, but you can't eliminate it.

But consider an analogy. For decades it was accepted as fact that serious accidents will happen at construction sites, especially when workers are dealing with inherently deadly products, such as electricity. But then Pieper Electric changed the perception. They made it their goal not only to reduce but to eliminate serious accidents at their worksites. And year after year they have achieved that goal. Once again, in 2011, with 625 employees, they reported 0 deaths, 0 days off from work, and 0 days of job transfer or restriction due to injury.

How do they do it?

They take safety seriously. They train their employees in the latest safety techniques. They evaluate safety. They reward safety. And they do all of this with a greater purpose. They want to eliminate serious accidents because they care about their employees. They live out their motto: "our people are our power."

Of course, Pieper Electric can't prevent all serious accidents in their community. They can only influence what happens on their worksites.

In the same way, preventing bullying in schools won't stop all violence against children. But it will stop some, and it will provide a place of safety for children who face violence at home.

Just as an electric company that cares about its employees won't tolerate unsafe working conditions, a society that cares about its children won't tolerate bullying in its schools.

Whether or not bullying is on the rise, it happens often

enough that adults should get serious about stopping it. It harms the children who are subjected to it, it harms the children who witness it, and it harms the children who do it.

If we care about our kids, we will make their safety our priority. And if it is our priority, it will become theirs as well.

June 3, 2012

67. STIGMA

It is curious how shameful events are impressed upon one's memory. I remember vividly the way kids in my elementary school singled out Jenny Kern for daily emotional abuse. Why did we pick on her? She was chubby, awkward, and her clothes were dirty.

If someone touched her, we said they got "Kern's germs." We were normal; she was not. We made her life hell.

The term "stigma" comes from a Greek word referring to a mark on the skin, such as a brand, tattoo, or piercing. By the Middle Ages, the term had come to be used in largely symbolic fashion, referring not only to visible marks, but any condition taken to be a "mark" of shame or disgrace.

The worse thing about stigma is that those who are stigmatized often come to internalize the shame, seeing themselves as outside the bounds of normal humanity.

There are many occasions for stigma—poverty, ethnicity, disfigurement, disease, mental illness—but they are occasions only and not causes. Stigma is connected to conditions from which people want to distance themselves. When we stigmatize someone, we attempt to establish an illusion of invulnerability, as if we ourselves were not also susceptible to misfortune.

For centuries people suffering from mental illness have been stigmatized.

According to the National Survey on Drug Use and Health, in 2011 45.6 million American adults (20% of the population) experienced some form of mental illness. Given the prevalence of the condition, it is remarkable that our society has so little understanding of what it is, how to talk about it, and how to embrace those who suffer from it.

The National Alliance on Mental Illness takes a wise posi-

tion on the topic of stigma. They do not object to the use of particular words like "crazy" or "loony," unless used to denigrate
people with mental illness. What they object to is language that
dehumanizes. "We protest calling a person a 'schizophrenic':
NAMI policy calls for PEOPLE FIRST: people, persons, individuals with a mental illness, schizophrenia, bipolar, clinical
depression, OCD, panic disorder."

Stigma is a form of injustice; it identifies a person with a
particular condition and in so doing obscures the person's humanity. "We" attempt to keep ourselves separate from "them"
by using language to create an emotional distance.

The only thing that removes stigma is empathy. Whenever
we identify with someone, we see him or her as a person like
ourselves and no longer as an object of fear or disgust. But this
is difficult to do. It is one thing to acknowledge someone's misfortune; it is another thing altogether to genuinely imagine that
we ourselves could be subject to that misfortune.

Simone Weil writes that justice begins when we imagine
our vulnerability: "I may lose at any moment, through the play
of circumstances over which I have no control, anything what-
soever that I possess, including things that are so intimately
mine that I consider them as myself. There is nothing that I
might not lose."

Every form of cruelty, brutality, nastiness, and injustice,
whether individual or institutional, comes from a failure to
acknowledge the radical contingency of our lives. We when
acknowledge that contingency, the barriers between "us" and
"them" cannot be sustained.

My attempt to keep an emotional distance from Jenny
proved short-lived.

My mother was the school nurse. She noticed what was
happening to Jenny and began inviting her to stop into her office in the morning. There she would discreetly wash Jenny's

face and hands and give her a hug and some encouragement.

One day after school my mother told me about Jenny's home life, how she lived in a little shack with no running water and how her parents could not afford to buy extra clothes. As she told me this I recalled the stories about my mother's childhood in similar conditions. She didn't say it, but I suspected that she had endured the same treatment as a child.

From then on I could not join in the teasing; I could not help but see Jenny as a person just like me, only perhaps a little more honorable in that she had never treated me cruelly.

March 10, 2013

68. Winning

The other day I heard a sports commentator remark about the Penn State scandal: "This isn't about football; it's about child sexual abuse."

His point was well-intended. He wanted to make sure that in all the controversy over Joe Paterno's firing and the ensuing protests by students, people remembered the victims.

And yet, the Penn State story did not make headlines because children were abused. Let's face it. There are approximately 800,000 substantiated cases of child abuse and neglect in the United States each year. How many of those stories are covered in the national news?

The Penn State story made national headlines because Joe Paterno is the winningest coach in the history of Division I college football. That's why ESPN has devoted two weeks of nearly non-stop coverage to this story. That's why it has been covered in this newspaper. That's why the commentator was talking about it that day. That's why I'm writing about it now.

Watching the mighty fall from grace is great entertainment, but it also gives us an opportunity for self-reflection. Joe Paterno is a heroic figure, and we look to heroes because we see ourselves in them. "All that Shakespeare says of the king, yonder slip of a boy that reads in the corner feels to be true of himself," observes Emerson.

When our heroes win, we share in their victories; when they lose, we share in their pain. But when our heroes betray our trust, we distance ourselves, and eventually we engage in a process of retrospective reexamination. Paterno is no exception. People are now saying that maybe he wasn't heroic after all: he was getting too old to head such a complex organization; he was a tyrant; he had a terrible temper.

In actuality, Paterno was a highly motivated, engaging, talented, and successful leader. He was probably more concerned with "results" than with what happened to people in the process of obtaining those results, but that's no different from many successful coaches. It's no different from many successful leaders in any type of organization.

The difference is that we wanted Paterno to be the exception. He's not just another coach. He's "JoePa," a father figure, someone we believed could both win and be a good man. Perhaps we even thought he must be a good man because he was winning.

It is not uncommon to conflate winning with morality. Think of what it means to say someone is a "good coach." Can a "good coach" have a losing record? Imagine a candidate for a head coaching job going into an interview saying, "I may not take this team to a championship, but I can guarantee you that the athletes will learn respect, integrity, and compassion." Such a candidate would be hard pressed to get hired by any self-respecting program.

"If winning isn't everything, why do they keep score?" asked Vince Lombardi. And he's got a point. Winning is the goal of sports. Just as making a profit is the goal of business. But that doesn't mean there aren't constraints, certain limits or boundaries within which winning may be legitimately pursued.

Winning and morality are not incompatible, but neither do they entail one another. What we really want from our heroes—whether they are coaches or athletes, business leaders or politicians—is both winning and morality. Because it is only when doing the right thing comes into conflict with the means of success that ethical character is tested and revealed.

The cost of not having a commitment to both winning and morality may be high, as we have seen in the scandal at Penn State. Those who pay the cost are frequently the innocent: most obviously and directly the victims of abuse, and also indirectly the athletes, students, and fans.

By Wednesday this past week, ESPN had moved on to a new top story: Mike Krzyzewski, men's basketball coach of the Duke Blue Devils, is now the winningest coach in NCAA history.

I wonder who the best coach is.

November 20, 2011

69. AUTHORITY

In response to the NCAA penalties levied against Penn State last week, the family of Joe Paterno issued a statement criticizing the NCAA for its reliance upon the Freeh Report: "to claim that [Joe Paterno] knowingly, intentionally protected a pedophile is false." Former Penn State president Graham Spanier, in a letter to the board of trustees, also criticized the report, claiming that he had no direct knowledge that sexual abuse of children was taking place on the campus.

Both Spanier and the Paterno family seem to think that responsibility requires knowledge, and that usually is the case when one is trying to determine individual responsibility for an action. But it is not the case for leaders of organizations. The Freeh Report addressed individual responsibility, but it focused primarily on institutional control. It asked why two janitors who witnessed abuse in 1998 were afraid to report it and why the university did not follow up appropriately in 2001 when Mike McQueary did report it.

In any organization, leaders bear responsibility not only for what they do, but for what they allow others under their authority to do. That's partly because leaders ought to know what is taking place under their watch, but it is also because of the ways authority influences behavior.

In 1961 Yale University psychologist Stanley Milgram conducted a series of experiments designed to determine whether ordinary people would obey an authority figure even if they were told to do something they knew to be wrong. This was a significant question because the Eichmann trial was taking place in Jerusalem that year. Adolf Eichmann, a Nazi officer in charge of transporting Jews to killing centers throughout Europe, defended his actions by saying he was just following orders. Milgram wanted to determine whether such a defense was plausible. If an ordinary citizen was placed in Eichmann's situation, would he or she do the same thing?

Milgram solicited volunteers for an experiment he claimed was designed to test the effects of electrical shocks on memory. He divided participants into two groups—the "teachers" and the "learners." The learners were charged with memorizing word pairs. The teachers were directed to say one of the words and ask the learner to recall the matching word. If the learner did not recall the right word, he or she would be given an electrical shock. The voltage was increased for each wrong answer. The volunteers did not realize that the learners were actually actors pretending to receive shocks. The experiment was intended not to test memory but to determine whether people would do something they knew to be wrong just because they were told by an authority figure to do so.

The results astounded Milgram. In his first set of experiments, 65% of the volunteers delivered shocks up to the maximum level, even after the learners pleaded with them to stop.

The Milgram experiments revealed that people in positions of authority wield an extraordinary amount of influence over those they supervise. That influence extends not only to people's actions but to how they perceive the rightness or wrongness of their actions. The subjects knew that causing pain to others was wrong, but because they were told by the researcher to continue, they persuaded themselves that they were not responsible.

Because the leaders of institutions create a culture within which some behaviors are encouraged, others tolerated, and yet others are condemned, they bear responsibility not just for what they know but for what other people within that culture do. At Penn State, the question is not simply whether the leaders knew for a fact that Sandusky was sexually abusing children. The significant question is why they failed to create a culture in which employees would be expected to put the safety of children before everything else.

The Freeh Report contends that the leaders at Penn State not only concealed information about allegations of sexual abuse, they also "provided Sandusky with the very currency that enabled him to attract his victims." Part of this currency was a moral economy in which those in authority neglected to empower those beneath them to act as responsible moral agents. Whether they were fully aware of the cost of their neglect is beside the point.

July 29, 2012

70. Concealed Carry

Folks in Wisconsin are up in arms over proposed concealed carry legislation, and yet, despite the arguments used on both sides of the debate, the issue is more about personal attitudes towards guns than legitimate concerns over public safety.

The Pew Research Center has been tracking public opinion on guns for the past eighteen years. In 1993, 57% of Americans thought it was more important to control guns than to protect gun owners' rights, while 37% thought gun rights were more important than gun control. In the latest survey last September, public opinion on gun control versus gun rights was split nearly 50–50.

However, what has remained constant over the past eighteen years is the demographic division on gun issues: 63% of people from rural areas favor protecting gun rights while only 38% of urban residents think gun rights are more important than gun control.

How are these statistics relevant to the Wisconsin debate over concealed carry? Well, the chief argument used by supporters of the legislation is that it will allow people to protect themselves from violent crime. And yet, the demographic divisions on the issue show that people who are most likely to actually need protection are the least likely to support the legislation. After all, according to the U.S. Department of Justice, the violent crime rate is 74% higher in urban areas than in rural areas.

Why do many people in urban areas tend to favor increased restrictions on handguns? Probably because their most common experience with guns is as victim of gun crimes. I lived for a total of 15 years in two of the most dangerous cities in the US—Baltimore and Memphis. During that time I met only a few people who had ever used a firearm, but nearly everyone I met had either been a victim or had family or friends who had been victims of crimes involving guns. I had two close friends who were robbed at gunpoint, a babysitter who was mugged in front of our house, and a neighbor who had his wallet stolen at gunpoint while tending his flower garden. The one time I found myself looking down the wrong end of a Browning 9mm I was delivering a casserole to the house next door.

Experiences such as these shape attitudes much more effectively than statistics. And if your experiences are all on one side (either as gun user or gun victim), your attitude toward guns is likely to be one-sided as well.

But statistics are important. They show that gun-related crimes do not increase as a result of relaxing restrictions. In fact, FBI reports show that in Florida, Texas, and Michigan, murder rates have paralleled a national downward trend since the introduction of right-to-carry laws. But in Chicago, which instituted a hand-gun ban in 1982, the murder rate has dropped less than the national average, and the percentage of murders committed with handguns has actually increased by 40%.

Opponents of concealed carry point out the increased risk of accidental shooting that comes from having more people in society armed. But when it comes to serious accidents, guns are a statistical non-factor.

In 2007 there were 613 accidental deaths from gunshot wounds in the U.S., but there were 23,443 deaths from falling, 40,059 poisoning fatalities, and 44,138 deaths involving motor vehicles.

In the end, I think the hoopla over concealed carry is overblown. There are so many factors to be considered in analyzing violent crime rates that we don't know if allowing people to carry handguns makes society slightly safer or slightly more dangerous; all we know is that the difference is slight.

If we are interested in making society safer, we would be well-advised to address the risks of driving, walking, eating, and drinking—things that most of us do frequently—rather than shooting—something which relatively few people do infrequently.

June 5, 2011

71. NRA

I was raised in the gun culture. I shot my first duck at age 10 with my grandmother's Winchester single shot .410. The next year I graduated to an Ithaca Model 37 20-gauge pump, and then went through a succession of hand-me-down shotguns until I finally saved enough to buy my own, a used Remington 870 Wingmaster. For my 12th birthday my grandpa Emmett gave me a Smith & Wesson .38 Special. He got it from his uncle, a law enforcement officer in San Francisco who confiscated it from a speakeasy during a federal raid. Every grandchild received a gun from Emmett on his or her 12th birthday.

All of the men and most of the women in my extended family own guns. As for many Americans, owning, shooting, talking about, and handling guns safely and responsibly has been an integral part of my life.

And so, when Wayne LaPierre, executive vice president of the National Rifle Association, delivered a defiant speech last week following the school shooting in Newtown, Connecticut, I understood his indignation.

But as he spoke, I was also reminded why the NRA does not speak for me and why a sizeable minority of lifelong gun owners are embarrassed to be represented by such an organization.

LaPierre said of the media that "they perpetuate the dangerous notion that one more gun ban—or one more law imposed on peaceful, lawful people—will protect us where 20,000 others have failed!"

Well, people in the media do say a lot of dumb things about guns, but LaPierre beat them to it with this one. There is no way he, or anyone else, can know whether existing gun restrictions have saved lives or not.

In order to demonstrate the link between cause and effect, researchers must isolate the phenomena under investigation. That is not always possible. So when someone states that studies have failed to show a link between, say, gun bans and gun violence or video games and school shootings, that may be because there is no connection or it could be that the relevant factors are complicated and inextricably entwined with other relevant factors.

The difficulty of demonstrating cause-effect relationships did not stop LaPierre from casting the blame for school shootings on violent entertainment, especially movies and video games. But the charge was disingenuous. Was he unaware of the close relationship between the NRA and the gaming industry?

A recent story in the New York Times pointed out that Electronic Arts created a website for one of its recent releases, Medal of Honor Warfighter, to promote products featured in the game. Among the companies advertised on the site was the McMillan Group, manufacturer of the CS5, a sniper rifle. McMillan is a corporate sponsor of the NRA.

As one would expect, gaming advocates deny that their products lead to a real-world culture of violence. Chris Sullentrop, author of a popular gaming blog, emphasized the point: "There's no evidence that video games cause—or even correlate with—violence, and that can't be stated often enough."

This does not mean there is no connection. I agree with LaPierre that there most likely is, but, to be honest, it is not as strongly established as the link between gun ownership and gun violence.

The gun-related homicide rate in the United States is approximately 3 people per 100,000. That compares to 0.3 per 100,000 in Western Europe, where gun ownership is negligible. The U.S. ranks #1 in the world in gun ownership, with about 9 guns for every 10 people. We rank #2 in the world for gun violence.

Such statistics do not prove that guns cause violence. But they do reveal a strong correlation, and correlations suggest a cause-effect connection that has yet to be determined.

I like guns. I enjoy hunting and target shooting. I also enjoy fishing, skiing, golfing, biking, and basketball.

I don't like restrictions on the things I enjoy. But if bikes, or fishing rods, or skis, were being used to harm people, I would have to accept the fact that stricter regulations on those things might be necessary to protect the vulnerable.

Guns are used to harm people. Gun owners, especially those of us who use them safely and lawfully, need to acknowledge that and accept responsibility for making sacrifices that can reduce the harm.

LaPierre does not think law-abiding gun owners should be asked to pay a price for harm done by others. But that is precisely what we should do.

It is the cost of living in a moral society.

December 30, 2012

72. MONSTERS

In 1774 Johann Wolfgang von Goethe wrote *The Sorrows of Young Werther*, in which a young man kills himself after the woman he loves rejects him. The novel, popular throughout Europe, had an unanticipated, regrettable effect: a number of young men committed suicide due to romantic despair, something virtually unknown before that time.

Human beings are instinctively imitative. We shape our lives according to the images that we ourselves invent. Those images provide us with new possibilities of emotion, action and reaction, creativity and destruction.

What images shape our lives in unanticipated, regrettable fashion today?

According to Wayne LaPierre, executive vice president of the NRA, they are the images placed into our homes by the purveyors of violent movies and video games, "a callous, corrupt, and corrupting shadow industry that sells and sows violence against its own people."

But what LaPierre failed to note is the extent to which all of us, he included, have been influenced by the media he condemned. Take, for example, the following remark, which has passed virtually unnoticed: "The truth is that our society is populated by an unknown number of genuine monsters— people so deranged, so evil, so possessed by voices and driven by demons that no sane person can possibly ever comprehend them."

Hannibal Lecter, the Joker, Darth Vader, Lord Voldemort: the most notorious villains of movies and books are indeed monsters. They are so far removed from humanity as to be incomprehensible. That is precisely what makes their hold over our collective imagination so pernicious.

But what does it mean to think of real people as "monsters?"

All ideas have a history, and this particular one can be traced back to Manichaeism, a religious view dating to the 3rd century in which everything that happens in the universe is shaped by two equally powerful forces of good and evil.

It provides a simple explanation for why people do bad things: it is because they have been contaminated by evil. And since good and evil are mutually exclusive, there is no point in trying to gain some sort of understanding. The only way to win a dispute with evil is by force.

The contemporary expression of Manichaeism is this: You can't reason with monsters like Adam Lanza; the only way to protect ourselves from them is to lock them up or kill them.

But human beings, even those who do monstrous things, are not monsters; they are human beings.

The first task of ethics is to describe the world correctly. True descriptions of fundamental things are crucial, because when it comes to finding practical solutions to problems, which laws or policies seem reasonable depends to a great extent on how they fit with the way we see the world.

How does this apply in the case of someone like Adam Lanza? Well, for starters, it reminds us that we should not simply dismiss him as a "monster." If we want to prevent future shootings, we should try to understand what motivated him, which means trying to understand how his actions may have seemed reasonable to him at the time.

Of course, this means we have to acknowledge that Lanza, and other young men who have committed mass murder like Eric Harris or Dylan Klebold, are perhaps much more like ourselves than we want to admit. This is not to excuse or minimize the terrible wrongs they committed; rather it is to face the fact that their wrongs are human wrongs, something to which any human being, given certain circumstances, say of mental illness, or distorted perception, or strong emotion, may be susceptible.

None of this leads us in a straightforward fashion towards a solution to school shootings, because there is no simple true answer to the question of why some people do terrible things to others. But there are many simple false answers. When it comes to phenomena that are widespread and enduring, the answers that point the finger at someone else and say, "It is their fault and none of mine," are generally among the false ones.

As long as we remain under the influence of a distorted picture of human nature, any reasonable solution will escape our grasp.

January 13, 2013

73. BOY SCOUTS

Michael told me recently that he is gay. A high school junior, I've known him and his family for many years. Hardly anyone is surprised by his announcement. What is surprising is what a non-event his coming out has been.

I asked Michael how his classmates reacted. "Most of them just kind of shrugged," he said. "Actually, it's made things easier. People seem to know who I am now and just accept that."

Sexual orientation is just not a big issue for most young people today.

That's probably why there has been such a warm public reception for NBA center Jason Collins, the first active major pro sports athlete to announce he is gay.

The seismic shift in public attitudes about homosexuality is mostly due to generational changes.

The Pew Center for People and the Press released a report in March revealing that 70% of people born after 1980 support same-sex marriage, approximately twice as many as those born before 1964.

That spells big trouble down the road for organizations that have made sexual orientation a defining issue.

A case in point is the Boy Scouts of America.

Later this month the National Council will vote on a proposal to alter its membership criteria. The crucial change is the addition of this sentence: "No youth may be denied membership in the Boy Scouts of America on the basis of sexual orientation or preference alone."

The BSA is stuck between a rock and a hard place.

If they vote the proposal down, they put the future of the organization at risk. Children born today are being raised by parents who largely regard sexual orientation as a matter of social diversity like race or gender and will not participate in organizations they perceive as intolerant.

If they pass the proposal, they put the present of the organization at risk. A large percentage of the BSA donor base comes from a generation that regards homosexuality as immoral and does not want to support an organization that encourages it.

It is difficult to "reason out" of a quandary like this, because most people's attitudes are based on emotion. Reasons are typically used to bolster and defend an emotional response, not create it.

Nevertheless, the reasons people give for opposing the change are revealing.

Many longtime supporters of scouting fear that changing the criteria for membership will have a drastic effect on the culture of the BSA. That fear is based in part on a false perception of the number of gay youth likely to join the scouts.

A Gallup survey conducted in 2011 revealed that most Americans estimate that 25% of the population is gay or lesbian. In reality, the percentage is closer to 3%. When you combine that percentage with the fact that many young men don't figure out their sexual orientation until high school or college age, it is easy to see that the proposed change in membership criteria would likely have a negligible effect on BSA culture.

Another concern is that allowing gay members might put youth at risk of sexual abuse. But the worry has no basis. When the BSA consulted leading national experts on this question, their consensus response was that "same-sex sexual interest or same-sex sexual experience, either in adults or youth, is NOT a risk factor for sexually abusing children."

For most of us, our moral attitudes are shaped by personal connections. If we know someone who is gay or lesbian, we are much more likely to be tolerant of their lifestyle, even if we do not agree with it.

Michael is not a concept; he is a person. I care deeply about him. I want him to have all the advantages that a loving family and strong social network can provide. I want him to discover his passion and develop the skills and habits that lead to a productive, fulfilling life. Organizations like the Boy Scouts are designed to do just that.

As Jason Collins said in an interview last week: "It doesn't matter that you're gay.... It's about working hard, it's about sacrificing for your team. It's all about dedication. That's what you should focus on."

If the Boy Scouts of America want to help kids like Michael, they need to focus on that as well.

May 5, 2013

74. MARRIAGE

In the summer of 1967 I was a ring-bearer in my aunt and uncle's wedding. Dressed up in a grey tuxedo with pin-striped vest, cuff links, tie pin, and shiny black shoes, I walked down the aisle with Suzy, the flower girl, and took a place at the front of the church. It was a Catholic wedding mass on a hot summer day. Halfway through the ceremony I fell asleep and tipped over into the groomsman next to me, disrupting the service.

Jack and DeeDee spent less than $1,000 on their wedding, the average cost in those days. Today a typical wedding costs $28,000. But that's not the only difference. My aunt and uncle were doing what most young adults did then: graduate from high school, get a job or go to college, get married, have a family. According to the Pew Center, 72% of adults 18 and over were married in 1960. Today, that number is 51%.

Of all the changes in American society over the last 50 years, the decline in marriage is the most troubling.

And yet, hardly anyone is talking about it. There is, instead, a great deal of debate about same-sex marriages.

The reality is that legalizing marriage for homosexual couples will not have much societal impact. What really matters is that heterosexuals, who comprise 97% of the population, are increasingly choosing not to get married.

I think the emotional intensity of the same-sex marriage debate reflects deep confusion over the nature and purpose of marriage. The roots of that confusion can be traced back two-thousand years.

Under classical Roman law, marriage was a civil contract. The Catholic Church reconceived marriage as a holy sacrament in which God joins a man and a woman together for the purpose of raising a family. Marriage became a metaphysical union, not just a contract.

In 1644, John Milton published *The Doctrine and Discipline of Divorce,* redefining marriage on the basis of companionship. Quoting the passage in Genesis in which God creates Eve as a cure for Adam's loneliness, Milton writes: "From which words so plain, less cannot be concluded...than that in God's intention a meet and happy conversation is the chiefest and the noblest end of marriage."

Milton's redefinition of marriage became the standard view in Protestant denominations, which since the Reformation had conceived of marriage not as a sacrament but as a covenant, a kind of hybrid between the classical Roman and Catholic conceptions of marriage.

In the United States today, in which approximately 50% of the population identifies as Protestant, 25% as Catholic, and the other 25% as other or no religion, there is a lack of consensus as to the nature and purpose of marriage.

Is marriage a civil contract, a holy sacrament, or a covenant? And what is its purpose? Is it a commitment to raise children, a state of companionship, or an agreement to share resources?

In the same-sex marriage debate, all of these questions come up. But while Americans are fond of taking sides on issues, we are not so fond of patiently discussing fundamental questions.

We need to have a national conversation about marriage, because as it stands now, the institution is slowly dying.

Several national studies point to the fact that married parents are key to raising children to be physically, emotionally, and financially secure.

Yet young couples are increasingly choosing cohabitation over marriage. Today 40% of children spend at least part of their childhood in a cohabiting household. Those children are ten times more likely to suffer physical abuse than children in a married household with biological parents.

An even greater concern is that children brought up by married parents are set upon on a path of upward socio-economic mobility, while the children of single and cohabiting parents face a downward future. Studies show this trend is creating two rapidly diverging classes in America: the poor unmarried class and the wealthy married class.

Jack and DeeDee had few financial resources when they got married. But they understood that their wedding wasn't a performance meant to impress; it was a public ritual of commitment, in which family and friends witnessed and pledged to help them keep their vows. They all knew that marriage is important for families, and that families are the basis of strong communities.

May 19, 2013

"Would you like to sign up for a Balance Rewards card?" the cashier asked. "You can save $1."

That's a good question, I thought. To save $1, all I have to do is provide my personal information and permission to track my purchases. Given all the ways corporations and government already obtain and store information about me, that's not much more of an intrusion into my life. Over the course of a year, it could add up. How much is that little bit of privacy worth? $1? $20? $100?

The erosion of the distinction between private and public is one of the defining features of our age. We find it in the ways the world enters into our homes through technology, in the omnipresence of cell phones, GPS in automobiles, computers in the kitchen and living room, in the ways our lives are recorded and displayed on social networking sites.

The issue of privacy came to the fore of public attention locally when the La Crosse City Vision Foundation announced plans to install forty-one security cameras to help police monitor illegal activity in downtown La Crosse.

Do security cameras pose a threat to privacy? They certainly could, but most people would agree that they do not, as long as they are clearly marked and installed in public places like parking ramps, streets, and alleys.

In interpreting the Fourth Amendment, the U.S. Supreme Court has used "the reasonable expectation of privacy" as a standard for determining what crosses the line. When security cameras are placed in areas where people are accustomed to being observed anyway, it is hard to claim that they violate one's expectation of privacy.

But as the use of advanced technology becomes more widespread, society's reasonable expectations may very well change. Is there a point at which we may reasonably expect no privacy at all?

The FAA Modernization and Reform Act of 2012 provides for the integration of drones in domestic airspace. If the use of drones for surveillance and other purposes by law enforcement, military, universities, and private corporations becomes widespread over the next few years, we may soon come to think of all outdoor spaces as non-private.

The transformation of indoor spaces is happening just as rapidly. Judging by the numbers of cell phones dropped in the toilet each year (well over a million), even the most private of private places is no longer off limits to social life in the digital age.

The real threat to privacy comes not from security cameras on public streets but from sources that are not so obvious, because they operate outside the bounds of our awareness. Even when consent is obtained, the ways in which information is manipulated can be so confusing that people are often unsure what they have agreed to.

An example is the Federal Trade Commission's recent report that it is investigating cellphone apps to determine whether they are being used to collect information on children and pass it on to third parties. How many parents know what information is being collected about their children, who possesses it, and what can be done with it?

Eric Schmidt, CEO of Google, remarked that "We don't need you to type at all. We know where you are. We know where you've been. We can more or less know what you're thinking about."

Privacy is important because it is the very basis of individuality. The ancient Greek word for "private" was *idios*, from which we get "idiot," "idiom," and "idiosyncratic." The private is that which is peculiar to the individual. One cannot be an individual without having something of one's own, whether that is property, behaviors, or thoughts. If everything is public, then nothing is truly "mine," everything becomes "ours."

The dire implications of our rapidly changing private-public boundaries have yet to be widely acknowledged because technology always outpaces our ethical intuition. It takes a long time for people to develop a shared sense of right and wrong because ethics is only partly a matter of analysis. It also requires experience.

Sometimes experience comes too late.

January 27, 2013

76. Drones

There have been incidents in America's wars about which we all feel remorse: the firebombing of Dresden at the close of World War II, which killed about 25,000 German civilians; the Mai Lai massacre, in which approximately 400 women, children, and elderly civilians were murdered in South Vietnam; or, closer to home, the Bad Axe Massacre, 180 years ago last week, in which over 400 members of the Sauk and Fox tribes were killed trying to cross the Mississippi River near Victory, Wisconsin..

No reasonable person can defend the intentional killing of civilians. But how do we feel about the unintended but foreseeable civilian deaths that occur routinely in military actions?

Collateral damage—the unintentional killing of civilians— has always been an inextricable part of warfare, and that has always been the chief reason why war is considered a last resort. But the situation is changing with the advent of robotic warfare.

Administration insiders say the use of drone strikes to assassinate terrorists is driven in large part by President Obama's commitment to the "just war theory," an ethical tradition dating from the middle ages that considers the use of force to be justified only in self-defense and only when taking every measure to insure that innocent people are not killed. Obama personally reviews potential targets and authorizes every name on the "kill list."

The number of civilian casualties resulting from drone strikes seems to be approximately 20%. That is a relatively low figure compared to collateral damage percentages in traditional military conflicts, which, according to a recent *New York Times* report, has ranged from 33% to 80% over the last twenty years.

Since President Obama came into office nearly eight years ago, the percentage of civilians killed in military strikes has decreased dramatically due to the effectiveness of drones in identifying and selecting intended targets.

But that doesn't mean fewer civilians are being killed. Precisely because the drones are so effective at reducing collateral damage, they are being used more frequently.

There are currently 57 drone combat air patrols in operation overseas, mostly in Pakistan, but also in Yemen and Somalia. Drone strikes now take place in Pakistan about once every four days.

According to the London-based Bureau of Investigative Journalism, the U.S. has carried out approximately 350 drone strikes since 2004, killing an estimated 3,500–4,000 people, including about 800 civilians.

These numbers are educated guesses, because neither the White House nor the Pentagon will provide statistics, and terrorist groups grossly exaggerate the number of civilian casualties.

In June a Pentagon spokesperson disputed estimates reported in *Newsweek,* but refused to provide an official number, saying only, "I can assure you that the number of civilian casualties is very, very low."

Paradoxically, the very effectiveness of drone strikes is what makes them morally problematic. Because the only people directly involved in the attacks are the victims, there is no way for the rest of us to witness the cost of the suffering that is being inflicted on our behalf. Because we do not share the risk, we can easily ignore the harm.

Do drone strikes make the world safer, or do they make the world more dangerous while making Americans safer? Would even more civilians die at the hands of terrorists if we were to discontinue drone attacks?

I don't know the answers to those questions, but what distresses me most is that even in an election year, I don't hear anyone asking them.

The use of force without consequences to the user is a dangerous thing. In this new age of robotic warfare, we need to pause and reflect not only on what the technology allows us to do to others, but also on what it is doing to us. Is it leading us into complacent acceptance of what ought to be a last resort?

August 12, 2012

77. Signs

A committee of the La Crosse Common Council has proposed a sign ordinance that would regulate various features of signs, such as size, placement, brightness, height, and so on. Many residents favor the sign proposal; many businesses oppose it. I would think it would be the other way around.

Sometimes the way we define a controversy determines our response to it. If we think of an issue in terms of quality of life versus economics, then we will think of it as residents versus business. But in La Crosse, our economy is inextricably linked with quality of life. So the question for the Common Council is simple: what kinds of signs will enhance our local economy?

The most attention-grabbing signs are not always the best for business. A couple of weeks ago I was driving through a small town in northern Minnesota and noticed a sign on the side of a café–gas station. It read: "Eat here. Get gas and worms." I'm sure the sign attracted lots of attention; I'm not so sure it attracted many customers. At any rate, I did not stop. I already had gas and worms.

If you are a La Crosse resident you probably don't pay much attention to the number, variety, and placement of signs because they are so familiar. It's like the clutter in our living rooms that goes unnoticed until a visitor drops in.

Most people like their own clutter, but dislike the clutter of others.

Our own clutter is comfortable; it's the natural byproduct of activity. Sometimes, of course, it gets to be too much. When you spend more time looking for a pen than writing, it's time to clean the desk.

When I see another person's clutter, I immediately think:

"He sure is lazy." When I survey my own clutter, I think: "I sure am busy."

Too many signs arranged haphazardly will make a city appear cluttered. But a city without signs is like a desk without papers: there's nothing going on there.

Ever notice that bedroom communities have very few signs? Zzzzzz.

Out-of-towners form a lasting impression of our city within the first 15 minutes of their visit. What they perceive is not so much particular buildings or features but rather what the German philosopher Gernot Böhme termed "atmosphere." People get a general mood or impression of a place first; later, when they've become accustomed to the area, their perception tends to become more focused and selective.

Signs are the means by which we find our way around. One function of signs is to convey specific information, usually by labeling, reminding, or directing. Another function of signs is to complement the built and natural environment by creating a positive atmosphere, that is, to make the city inviting and attractive, especially for visitors.

A city that conducts business strictly among residents only has to worry about the first function of signs; a city that relies on attracting outsiders, whether they be tourists, shoppers, students, or conference goers, must be concerned also—and primarily—with the ways signs contribute to the atmosphere of the city.

There are places where signs create an intentional atmosphere—where they are meant to draw attention to themselves—places like Las Vegas or Times Square in Manhattan. But La Crosse is not such a place. I've never heard a tourist say, "You have such attractive signs here!"

Visitors are generally impressed with La Crosse: they love the historic downtown; they love the river; they love the bluffs.

But before they see any of those things they have to travel through the cluttered corridors that serve as entry ways into the city. And even though we residents may feel perfectly comfortable with them, they don't make a good first impression.

The sign ordinance proposal would establish guidelines to ensure that signs complement rather than detract from their natural surroundings. It is a fairly simple either-or proposition. If we care about bringing in business from visitors, we clean up our clutter. If we don't care about that, we leave it the way it is. After all, once you live here a while, you don't even notice it.

August 26, 2012

78. Capital Punishment

In a previous column I referred to the case of Teresa Lewis, a woman currently on death row in Virginia, as an example of the sort of punishment that we ought to find morally outrageous. I did not offer any reasons to support that claim, however, since the main point of that column was to look at how we make cross-cultural moral judgments. In the present column I turn to the topic of capital punishment explicitly, in order to examine its moral status.

When examining whether any kind of action is morally acceptable, there are four approaches one can take. First, one can look at the truth of the action, whether what is happening is properly understood and whether it is described correctly and completely. Secondly, one can look at the consequences of the action, in order to determine whether it has overall positive or negative effects on people. Third, one can look at the fairness of the action, to see whether it treats people equally and with respect. Fourth, and finally, one can look at the character with which the action is done, in order to assess the motivations of the people performing the action. Any credible moral reason that someone advances for or against any action uses one of these four approaches.

Let's take each approach in turn.

Truth: Capital punishment is a practice that depends upon deception for continued support. This wasn't always the case in the United States. At one time executions were carried out in the public square, and part of the deterrent effect was thought to be the publicity of the event. But now executions are carried out behind closed and locked doors and at times deliberately chosen to reduce public visibility. If more people witnessed the executions we wouldn't tolerate them, because we couldn't bear what intentional killing does to the witnesses.

Consequences: One of the arguments often given in support of the death penalty is that the state shouldn't have to pay for keeping a convicted murderer alive. But, in fact, the death penalty costs more, sometimes much more, than life in prison. A recent study in the state of Washington found that death penalty cases cost an average of $600,000 more per case than trying similar crimes as non-capital cases. This summer the Legislative Services Agency in the state of Indiana compared the cost of capital cases to the cost of life-without-parole cases. The former averaged $449,887; the latter averaged $42,658. This year the state of California is cutting back on homicide investigations because of their budget crisis while continuing to spend $137 million per year trying death penalty cases. Meanwhile, there is no credible evidence that the death penalty has a deterrent effect. It is just as likely to increase violent crime.

Fairness: In the United States approximately 2% of convicted murderers are sentenced to death, but the nature of the crime committed has little to do with who receives the death penalty. Instead, the people who are executed tend to be those who have killed a white person and received incompetent legal representation. In 2001 Supreme Court Justice Ruth Bader Ginsburg observed: "I have yet to see a death case among the dozens coming to the Supreme Court on eve-of-execution stay applications in which the defendant was well represented at trial." Even a cursory glance at the evidence reveals that, whatever the merits of the death penalty, it is being implemented arbitrarily.

Character: Here we come to the crux of the issue. The reason capital punishment has so much support in this country is that it is motivated by vengeance. And that is certainly understandable. When I imagine myself in the position of a victim or victim's family, I want to see the perpetrator punished severely.

Any person would. But the state is not a person. The obligation of the state is not to see that vengeance is satisfied, but that justice is carried out. It has to ensure that both the investigation and the prosecution of a crime are conducted dispassionately, reliably, and fairly.

I tend to agree with proponents of the death penalty that murderers deserve to die, but lots of people deserve things that the state cannot effectively provide and that taxpayers shouldn't be expected to pay for. So until we find a way to carry out capital punishment truthfully, effectively, fairly, and justly, you can put me down as opposed.

August 29, 2010

79. NUCLEAR POWER

On March 20, a spokesperson for the Nuclear Regulatory Commission stated that "the NRC remains confident that our Reactor Oversight Program, which includes both on-site and region-based inspectors, is effectively monitoring the safety of U.S. nuclear power plants." A few days earlier Energy Secretary Stephen Chu proclaimed that "the American people should have full confidence that the United States has rigorous safety regulations in place."

It is an interesting choice of words. The government has confidence in their programs and inspectors; the public is asked to have confidence in the government.

"Confidence" means, literally, "shared faith." To have faith in someone is to trust them with something important—a vital secret, one's health, one's retirement account, one's children, one's life.

Some people associate faith exclusively with religion. But the idea that faith consists of holding certain religious beliefs is a misleadingly narrow conception. Faith is not simply or even primarily a matter of belief. Faith implies a trusting relationship, not mental certainty. Like all virtues, the test of it lies in a person's actions.

Some religious and political leaders make agreeing with beliefs more important than the quality of one's actions, an emphasis that is warranted neither by sound theology nor good politics. This misplaced emphasis on belief leads to the misconception that the opposite of faith is doubt.

Faith has two corresponding vices, a vice of excess and a vice of deficiency. The vice of excess is gullibility—being too ready to place control in the hands of another who is not necessarily trustworthy. The vice of deficiency is skepticism—an unwillingness to trust regardless of merit.

The gullible person is not interested in asking difficult questions. To him, the fact that government officials declare nuclear plants safe is evidence enough. When critics bring up radioactive waste storage, he changes the subject, insisting simply that we need nuclear plants to keep energy affordable.

The skeptic won't take yes for an answer. If new and safer plant designs are proposed, she doesn't want to consider them. She will point to Japan and Three Mile Island and Chernobyl. She refuses to trust without having absolute proof that things will turn out well, but that standard of certainty is never possible.

In many cases, people prove worthy of our faith in them. Those who grow and inspect our food, build and repair our airplanes, teach our children, and ensure the quality of our drinking water, generally do a good job. Sometimes accidents happen or oversights occur, but, for the most part, our daily practical confidence in those who are responsible for public safety is warranted.

But nuclear power is different. Not just because the potential for human catastrophe is greater, but because it is on a scale that human beings cannot comprehend.

I trust the government when it says that current nuclear power plants have safety standards and policies in place that make it very unlikely for a nuclear meltdown to occur in the next ten to twenty years. But when it says we can safely produce thousands of tons of radioactive waste for our grandchildren and great-grandchildren to dispose of, they are talking about something they have no ability to comprehend.

Predictions about what will happen with radioactive waste in the distant future are based on assumptions (environmental, economic, political, and technological) that are unknown and unknowable.

The energy company that proposes to build a plant producing 10,000 years of radioactivity for 30 years of energy is like a church that promises eternal life in return for $100 in the offering plate.

How do we know when to place our faith in someone? There is no rule for that, no foolproof set of guidelines or instructions, just as there are no sure guidelines for how to act courageously, or temperately, or wisely, or justly. But a good rule of thumb is not to trust someone whose promises are out of all proportion to their capacity to deliver.

March 27, 2011

80. Organ Donation

If a miracle becomes commonplace, is it still a miracle?

Every day 79 people receive organ transplants. Yet unless the recipient happens to be, say, a former vice president, the story doesn't make the headlines. It doesn't even make the back pages.

Still, it is a miracle to the recipient and to those who love him or her. When someone has been waiting for months under a sentence of death because of failing kidneys, or heart, or lungs, the sudden appearance of a match—the right tissue type, at the right time, in the right place—seems like a miracle. Life is possible again.

In the past, the success of organ transplantation was limited by technology. Keeping matched organs viable until surgery, incidents of infection, and subsequent rejection of transplanted organs all presented significant obstacles. But in recent years incredible advances have been made. It is not unusual for a heart transplant recipient to live a productive life for ten years or more.

These days the chief limitation on transplantation is availability of organs. In the United States, 18 people die every day on the waiting list. If more people registered to be donors, more lives could be saved.

Why don't more people sign up to be organ donors? The reasons are many, but they come down to two factors: ignorance and reluctance.

Many people falsely believe they are registered as an organ donor even though they are not. Simply signing up at the DMV and receiving a driver's license with the little orange "donor" circle is not sufficient. One must also sign up with the state organ donation registry. In Wisconsin and Minnesota, that's a simple matter of going to www.donatelifemidwest.org and filling out the online form. It takes about three minutes.

It is also important to talk to one's family about one's intention to be a donor so that in the event of an unexpected death one's family does not have the burden of making a difficult decision about something they haven't already considered.

But the chief obstacle to registering is probably a reluctance on the part of potential donors to fully imagine their own death and to make practical decisions about what to do when that time comes.

If I register as an organ donor I am agreeing to give up the part of me I most closely identify with: my body. And that's vastly different from agreeing to give up my possessions. To agree to be an organ donor is to acknowledge the inevitability and finality of one's death.

And yet, that is one of the most significant things about it. Everybody finds it hard to acknowledge that when it comes to that which we value most—life itself—we have no ultimate control. But that is a fact, and it's important to face it and discuss it with those we love.

The act of registering to be an organ donor—the decision to give one's body to save another's life—means acknowledging a good that persists beyond my personal interest. It is, in the end, an act of hope, because genuine hope only comes when we give up our individual concerns and commit ourselves, body and soul, to the good of others. In this way, hope is grounded in love.

Organ donation advocates often wish to impress upon potential donors the very great need that exists and also the immense gratitude that recipients feel. Yet, to my mind, an even greater motivation extends from the simple fact that the gifts are already in place—that if I or one of my loved ones were to sustain a significant injury to a vital organ, strangers have already said, in effect, "Here, take. This is my body; I give it to you."

Such generosity is breathtaking. How can I not be willing to do the same?

April 8, 2012

81. Don't Worry

Sometimes I think I worry too much. So lately I've been listening to happy songs.

When Bobby McFerrin recorded "Don't Worry, Be Happy" nearly a quarter century ago it touched a chord (so to speak) with listeners. It reached #1 on the Billboard charts and earned McFerrin several Grammies.

The song is simple—some would even say simplistic—but its wisdom is timeless: "In every life we have some trouble, when you worry you make it double."

The same sentiment was voiced by Montaigne in the 16th century: "He who fears will suffer; he already suffers from his fear."

The apostle Paul was especially clear upon this point: "Have no anxiety about anything," he wrote.

And the Stoic philosopher Epictetus, writing in the 2nd century, said: "What upsets people is not things themselves but their judgments about the things."

The truth in such words is not just idle speculation; it is empirically supported.

The past few years have seen a virtual explosion in research on the nature and causes of happiness. One thing nearly all the research agrees upon is that the primary source of anxiety is over a future that may or may not come to pass. When people are asked how they are doing right at the moment, most say they are doing just fine.

Of course, bad things do happen. It isn't wise to ignore problems in the blind hope that they will go away, but worrying about them doesn't make things better. In fact, it makes things worse.

People who are afraid make really bad choices about how

to address problems. They tend to see everything in black and white terms, and they become oblivious to other ways of thinking. So if you want to make good choices about the future, you need to stop worrying. That's the first step. Then you can think realistically about how to make things better.

Whether we are talking about families, politics, or economics, the causes of function and dysfunction are largely the same: attitudes reinforce themselves and shape behavior. If we believe we can make things better and work toward that result, we generally succeed. Human beings are an extraordinarily creative, industrious, and adaptable species.

In *Upside: Surprising Good News about the State of Our World,* University of Connecticut sociologist Bradley Wright analyzes data from the around the world regarding infant mortality, poverty, disease, and the environment. The result? By nearly every objective measure, the Beatles were right: you've "got to admit it's getting better, a little better all the time."

But we do have one problem. Occasionally, for some reason or another, we begin telling ourselves that the problems are overwhelming. And we talk ourselves into making it so.

Why is the economy stuck in a rut? Because even though corporations have accumulated huge stockpiles of cash they are not creating new jobs. And why are they not investing in new jobs? Because of anxiety about the future state of the economy. And why are they worried about the future economy? Because unemployment is so high. See the problem?

John Maynard Keynes, who advised the Roosevelt administration during the Great Depression, understood that economic performance is a matter of confidence more than anything else. Focusing too much on what we cannot afford is unhealthy. The only way to turn around a poor economy is to invest. When people think things are getting better, they invest. When people think things are getting worse, they withhold.

Our worries keep us from accomplishing as much as we could. So we need to count our blessings, to continually remind ourselves that things are better than they seem.

If you want to do your part in making the world a better place, just go to your favorite music site and pick up "Don't Worry, Be Happy." Listen once before reading the newspaper, going to a meeting, or watching the evening news. If that hasn't improved your attitude after one week, add a dose of Bob Marley's "Three Little Birds" before going to bed, and "don't worry 'bout a thing, 'cause every little thing gonna be all right."

November 6, 2011

PEOPLE

82. Heroes

One of the highlights of my year is reading nominations for the *La Crosse Tribune* Person of the Year. What stands out is not just the extraordinary goodness of a few people but the basic everyday goodness of so many.

Those who are nominated are not celebrities, and they are not "heroes," at least not in the sense we are accustomed to using that word. They haven't set any world records; they haven't saved dozens of lives in the battlefield; they haven't resolved a world conflict. But they have gone out of their way to be helpful to others, and they have been unusually dedicated and successful at doing so.

The nominations are submitted out of love, admiration, and gratitude. That itself reveals something about the people we most deeply respect: they are the people we know, not the celebrities we see only on TV.

This year the Person of the Year selection process coincided with the news that Ryan Braun, Milwaukee Brewers left fielder and National League MVP, had tested positive for using performance-enhancing drugs.

Ryan Braun is a poor role model for kids, not because he cheated but because the kids who admire him for his achievements cannot also observe the person who is not in the spotlight: the person who practices every day, who studies film, who lifts weights, and also, most importantly, deals with difficulties and setbacks.

For the same reason, football stars like Aaron Rogers and Tim Tebow are poor role models. Not because we may discover some skeleton in their closets, but simply because we don't know anything about their closets.

The best role model for a child is not a saint or hero, but

someone with whom the child can identify and emulate. And that requires a certain degree of familiarity. For that reason the best role models tend to be extended family members, teachers, coaches, or neighbors.

This is not to say that celebrities cannot be good role models. Sports figures like Tim Tebow or Aaron Rogers may be exemplary role models for their nieces and nephews, or for kids in their neighborhoods—that is, when they have an ongoing, regular presence in the life of someone. But they cannot be effective role models for thousands of kids. It just doesn't work that way.

The problem with having celebrities as role models is that we don't get to see what goes into the achievements. We don't get to see their private lives—their struggles, their preparation, the boring everyday stuff that makes up the majority of a person's life.

In *Soul of a Citizen* Paul Loeb recounts listening to a radio interview with Rosa Parks in which she was introduced as the black woman who one day refused to go to the back of the bus and thus set in motion the civil rights movement. But this description, Loeb points out, is misleading. Rosa Parks had spent years preparing for that moment by educating herself about civil rights, attending meetings, and leading a local NAACP chapter. The real story of Rosa Parks isn't the one act on the bus, it is the years of activity that led to an occasion when her refusal to move would have national significance.

When we focus too much on spectacular achievements, we tend to forget about all the hard, boring, non-spectacular work that makes those achievements possible. And we fail to give children a true depiction of how to become really good at something. After all, one isn't simply born into greatness. One becomes a Rosa Parks or an Aaron Rogers slowly, patiently, over many hours and days and years.

Perhaps in a celebrity-infatuated, media-saturated culture, we are simply not used to paying attention to the everyday goodness that makes our communities thrive. But when we do pay attention by nominating our neighbors, friends, and co-workers for recognition, it reminds us that we are surrounded by goodness, much of it hidden in plain sight.

January 1, 2012

83. Mame

I was having an engaging conversation with a young man recently when he asked, sincerely, "Why should I care about what happens to someone else?"

Questions like this can leave one speechless because we generally don't bother even to ask them. We just take it for granted that "good" people do care about others, "bad" people do not, and that most people fall somewhere between the extremes of selfishness and generosity, or narcissism and compassion.

But when someone actually asks the question, it is surprisingly difficult to answer. Is it possible to give a convincing reason why one should care for others?

The 18th century Scottish philosopher David Hume didn't think so. He maintained that compassion is something most people naturally feel for others, but there is no reason to be given for it. If someone is born without sympathy, nothing can be said to convince them to feel otherwise.

I don't entirely agree with Hume. I think it is possible to make an argument for compassion, but it is not a simple matter. It would have to be an argument from example: a case of comparing the lives of those who do and those who do not care about others and seeing which kind of life one would rather lead.

One day I met a man at a boat landing. He was taking his jet ski out of the river while I was waiting to launch my boat. He motioned for me to come over to his truck, flipped down the sun visor in the cab and said, "Take a look at this." There were five Rolex watches strapped to the visor. He was expecting me to be impressed. But all I could think was, "This poor guy must not have any friends if he is so eager to impress a stranger with trinkets."

Next door to my grandparents in a dilapidated house there lived an old woman named Mame who gave piano lessons to children. Some of the kids paid for their lessons, but for kids whose families couldn't afford it, the lessons were free. Every summer she hosted a party on her birthday and sent invitations to all the children in the neighborhood. She had cake and balloons and lots of music. When she died and her family came to clear out the house, I was surprised to notice that all her possessions fit into a little trailer. She had been so generous and full of life that abundance always seemed to surround her.

It is difficult to argue that caring for others is something one should do, but it is easy to point out that generosity and compassion are in fact characteristics of people who have rich and fulfilling lives. The most persuasive moral arguments are there to be seen in the lives of people we meet every day.

That is why we should take time to reflect on the lives of the really generous and compassionate people we encounter, in order to see how much better our lives could be if we would take a few little steps to act more like them. Repeated actions turn into habits; habits shape character; and character determines the quality of one's life.

Especially during this time of year, when every day is filled with frenzied preparations for gift-giving, and appeals from charities become ever more urgent, it is good to remember the people we have known, like Mame, whose life was rich because she nurtured loving relationships with others. After all, as my father-in-law is fond of saying, "there are no saddlebags on a coffin."

December 4, 2011

84. MOTHER'S DAY

Ding! No matter how hard I tried, I couldn't take the lid off my grandma's cookie jar without making that sound. Then her voice would shout from the other room. "Are you eating cookies again? It's only an hour 'til dinner time!"

For years I resented that tell-tale cookie jar—and my grandma's scrutiny, which never seemed to let up. Even after going off to college and settling down with my own family, the memory of her voice was a constant presence. "You're not going to waste your money on that, are you?" "Wipe your feet before you come traipsing through the house." "Didn't anyone teach you how to say 'please'?"

Not until many years after my grandma had passed away did it occur to me that her prohibitions were only one side of the story. I hadn't paused to appreciate the fact that the sugar cookies were always freshly baked for me.

I guess that's why we need Mother's Day. Some of us are so thick-headed, we need to be compelled into acknowledging the goodness—however imperfectly expressed—of those who raised us. The constraints on one's freedom that are naturally resented in youth require the perspective of age to be appreciated and forgiven. Until that time gratitude needs the encouragement of social pressure.

Mother's Day was originally proposed by Julia Ward Howe shortly after the Civil War. But the idea didn't really catch on until Anna Jarvis launched a zealous campaign to get the attention of churches and the legislature. It was signed into law in 1914 by President Woodrow Wilson. As it grew in popularity, however, Jarvis came to resent the commercialization of the holiday by florists and card makers and began organizing protests against it.

My favorite mother story comes from Ben Logan's *The Land Remembers,* his account of growing up on a farm near Gays Mills in the 1930s. On winter evenings the family would gather around the dining room table—the kids doing their homework, the father calculating the amount of seed or fertilizer he would need for the upcoming season, the mother mending clothes— all of them brought close by the circle of light emanating from an old Rayo kerosene lamp.

When his father brought home a new lamp the bright white light illuminated every corner of the room.

> I remember Mother standing in the doorway to the kitchen one night, frowning in at us. "I'm not sure I like that new lamp."
>
> Father was at his usual place at the table. "Why not? Burns less kerosene."
>
> "Look where everyone is."
>
> We were scattered. There was even enough light to read by on the far side of the stove.
>
> "We're all here," Father said.
>
> "Not like we used to be."
>
> Father looked at the empty chairs around the table. "Want to go back to the old lamp?"
>
> "I don't think it's the lamp. I think it's us. Does a new lamp have to change where we sit at night?"
>
> Father's eyes found us, one by one. Then he made a little motion with his head. We came out of our corners and slid into our old places at the table, smiling at each other, a little embarrassed to be hearing this talk.
>
> Mother sat down with us and nodded. "That's better."

Logan was fortunate to have a mother who understood the importance of constantly attending to the rituals of family life and also communicating that importance to her children in ways that were inviting. As parents we discover how difficult a task that is, through our own bumbling and partial attempts to maintain the conditions of genuine intimacy in which children flourish.

The motivations for celebrating Mother's Day may not be entirely pure, but then neither is the love between parents and their children. And that is why, despite Anna Jarvis's ambivalence, it is entirely appropriate that we celebrate Mother's Day with flowers: first, because all flowers are beautiful, when viewed in a certain light; second, because they are temporary. You know that you have to enjoy them today. Before you know it they are gone, and you have only the memory of how they could brighten a room.

May 8, 2011

85. Mom

*Where do we find ourselves? In a series of which we do
not know the extremes, and believe that it has none. We
wake and find ourselves on a stair; there are stairs below us,
which we seem to have ascended; there are stairs above us,
many a one, which go upward and out of sight.*
　　　　　　—Ralph Waldo Emerson, "Experience"

Last week my mother fell down a stairway. She fractured her
skull and sustained severe bruising to the left temporal lobe of
her brain. Nonresponsive for several days, she recently awoke
to a confusing world of faces she cannot place and words she
cannot comprehend. She can smile and point and say a few
simple words like "hi" and "okay." Mostly, she looks perplexed.

The left temporal lobe is the area of the brain that controls
speech, comprehension, and long-term memory.

To be without memory is to be cut-off, not just from one's
past, but from one's enduring connections with others. And in-
somuch as one's identity consists of relationships with others,
to lose one's memory is to lose a significant portion of one's
identity.

The ancient Greek philosopher Plato claimed that all knowledge is a function of memory. To know something is not simply
to believe it, but to recognize it. Likewise, to know a person is not
merely to be informed about who he or she is, but to be familiar
with the person, and then to be able to recall the circumstances
of that familiarity.

To know something is thus to remember it, to establish
once again one's relationship to the thing in question, to be
connected to it. To know other people is to establish and then
sustain a relationship, which we do primarily through words.

Words are so important to human relationships that without a common language spending time together is difficult. St. Augustine, the fourth century Catholic bishop, observed that it is easier to sit in a room with a dog than with a fellow human being who doesn't share the same language.

The word "conversation" (from the Latin *convertere*, literally "to turn together") originally meant something like "way of life." Over the centuries its meaning was reduced to simply "talking together," presumably because so much of our lives is taken up with forming and sustaining meaningful relationships through words. Talking together is how we connect and then reconnect with each other. We greet, debate, inquire, apologize, encourage, and condole. We catch up over coffee, participate in meetings, tell jokes, and listen to stories. Words are the means by which we shape communal life.

I don't know if my mother will regain her ability to speak clearly and coherently. The injury to her brain was so severe that she will most likely always struggle to some extent with speech and comprehension. But the more important question is: will she remember her children and grandchildren?

Perhaps not. But we can remember for her. We can remake and then work to sustain the connections that bind us together. That's the gift of community—that others may do what the individual cannot. By spending time, initiating her into the little rituals that comprise daily life, she may once again find her place. Not exactly the same place she occupied before, but maybe something close to it, and with its own share of significance.

The task before my family is a microcosm of the task perpetually facing humanity. Our basic moral obligation to one another is always to re-member, to put back together, to "make whole," insofar as that is possible. Whenever someone has experienced a significant loss, whether caused by accident, violence, betrayal, or natural disaster, doing what is right consists of trying to put lives back into some kind of order.

Building does not come as easily as tearing down. To re-member takes time. All the time in the world.

July 10, 2011

We remember people. And the memories reside in places.

The week began with news that my father-in-law, Byron Akers, passed away in Colorado Springs. It ended with conflagration, witnessing the burning of the landscape and landmarks that he had loved and become a part of over the course of his life.

The funeral took place Friday; the Waldo Canyon fire erupted the next afternoon. As we left to drive home on Sunday morning, ash was falling on the city.

The funeral, like the fire, was a reminder of how fragile we are—not just our mortal bodies, but the projects we commit ourselves to, the places we reside, and the things we love.

Byron was born in Colorado Springs in 1930. His father was editor of the *Gazette Telegraph*. His mother was an entrepreneur. She created the Pikes Peak Ghost Town Museum, one of many businesses in the area threatened both directly by the fire and indirectly by the collapse of tourism.

He and his wife LaVerne raised their family in the Rockrimmon area, near the Air Force Academy, adjacent to the fire's northern edge. They retired to a house overlooking the Garden of the Gods. The neighborhood has been evacuated.

The cause of the fire has not been determined, but arson has not been ruled out. Earlier in the week 20 fires were started by a suspected arsonist in adjacent Teller County. All of them were effectively extinguished. The Waldo Canyon blaze grew too quickly to be put out.

That which takes years to build may be destroyed in minutes. The Flying W Ranch was one of the first places to go. It started in 1953 with simple chuck wagon dinners and grew into an old-time western show, complete with a frontier town, live music and bad jokes, like "A three-legged dog came wandering into Dodge City. He walked up to the sheriff and said, 'I'm lookin' for the man who shot my paw.'"

When residents are evacuated from their homes the first thing they collect are family photos. Photos are how we remember who we are, evidence of connections to those who belong to us and to whom we belong. They are markers of significant occasions in our lives: births, graduations, weddings, anniversaries. We display photos at funerals. They tell the stories of our lives.

In his book *Blood and Belonging*, Michael Ignatieff reports how armies who wish to erase a people destroy their museums. Walking into a museum in Jasenovac in 1991, during the Serbo-Croatian conflict, he describes what he sees: "Every book in the library has been ripped up and tossed onto the floor. Every glass exhibit case has been smashed. Every photograph has been defaced." To destroy the memory of a people, one destroys the places where those memories reside.

But there is more to any life than can be summed up in memories. To attempt to describe a person's life adequately is, as Emerson says, to paint lightning with charcoal.

It is hard to know how many people Byron influenced during the course of his life. There would be no way to get an accurate count; I'm sure he didn't know himself. He had so many ways of helping people, with personal and professional advice, legal assistance, references, jobs, and finances. He was a man of considerable resources who used them generously and unselfconsciously.

In the end, good people are more endurable than the places they inhabit, the things they produce, or the artifacts that record their presence. They live on in the lives of those they influence. Their character traits, passed down from generation to generation, continue to find expression in the activities of daily life.

Because, after all, places have to be rebuilt. And they are rebuilt by good people who have learned from other good people how to work, and laugh, and play, and love.

July 1, 2012

87. SAM HARRIS

It was fifty years before Sam Harris was able to tell his story.

When Sammy was four years old, the Nazis invaded his hometown of Deblin, Poland. The town was turned into a ghetto and later into a concentration camp. He hid behind a pile of bricks while his parents, brothers, and four of his sisters were loaded onto railcars and shipped to gas chambers. With the help of two remaining sisters, he survived by hiding in the barracks for six years, escaping notice of the guards.

In 1948, at age 13, he was adopted by a couple from Chicago. And from that point on, he did everything he could to forget the child who lived through horror.

At night he would have nightmares and cry in his sleep. His mother would come into his room, sit on the edge of the bed, and cry with him. But she never asked him to talk about it.

His best friends at school knew only that he had been born in Europe. A popular student, he was elected class president, graduated, and went on to a successful career in insurance, fell in love, got married, had a family. He had put his past behind him.

One day his wife, Dede, came home from work, sat down at the kitchen table, and said: "It's time. Tell me about that little boy Sammy." And he did.

With Dede's encouragement, he came to see that Sammy wasn't the dirty, skinny, ignorant boy he had tried all those years to forget, but rather a brave and resourceful boy who had looked down the barrels of Nazi guns, had faced terror and death, and found a way to survive it all. She helped him bring the boy and the man back together. "I became whole," said Sam.

The Hebrew phrase *tikkun olam* means "repairing the world."

That is what Holocaust survivors do by telling their stories. If survivors' stories were just about the horror of the camps, nobody could bear to hear them. But they rarely are. Nearly always they are stories of perseverance, strength, hope, and, ultimately, of love.

In 1940, shortly after the Nazis invaded France, Simone Weil wrote an essay on Homer's *Iliad*—or, as she called it, "the poem of force." It is a powerful reflection on war and what happens to both victims and perpetrators of violence.

"Such is the power of force," wrote Weil. "Its power of converting a man into a thing is...double-edged. To the same degree, though in different fashions, those who use it and those who endure it are turned into stone."

She goes on: "Whoever, within his own soul and in human relations, escapes the dominion of force is loved."

Sam's inner strength allowed him to survive. He had to detach, as he put it, "to build a cement wall around my head." But that kind of strength preserves only a fragment of the soul. It does not permit one to be a whole person, connected with others in meaningful ways.

The love of others helped him regain his full humanity. First with his adoptive mother and then with his wife, Dede, he allowed himself to be vulnerable.

When Jesus said, "unless you change and become like little children, you will never enter the kingdom of heaven," I imagine he was talking about this very thing: only those who are willing to accept their radical dependence on the goodness of others can recover their humanity.

Violence dehumanizes. To survive its immediate effects one must harden oneself. But to live again, one must open oneself to the presence of others.

Love alone can restore humanity to both the victims and the wielders of force.

The stories of Holocaust survivors are inspiring because they bear witness to the endurance of the human spirit. "If he can survive that, then surely I can survive whatever life throws my way."

But that is only part of the message. What's more significant is that people like Sam Harris didn't merely survive; they managed to live a fully human life. They went on to love and be loved.

Thank you, Sam, for teaching us how to repair the world.

April 21, 2013

88. GERDA WEISSMAN KLEIN

Like many others, I have been disturbed recently by the political mood in our country, a mood that seems more often than not to be pessimistic, angry, and cynical.

Moods are infectious. They can creep into a society and transform it from within, altering perceptions, words, actions, policies, and laws.

America is ill-suited to dark moods. This country has had its share of difficult times, but the characteristic response of America is to face difficulties head on, to find a way forward, to find a silver lining in every cloud, not a cloud in every silver lining.

That is one reason it is so important to listen to people like Gerda Weissman Klein, holocaust survivor and author of *All But My Life*. She knows what real darkness is like—she lived through it and continues to live with its consequences. She makes a choice every day not to let darkness defeat her. And now she dedicates her remaining years to sharing her message.

What is that message? In a program she founded called Citizenship Counts, she reminds school children that American citizenship is a privilege, and like any privilege, it carries responsibilities.

That's an important message for children, but it is just as important for adults.

The way in which Ms. Klein delivers her message is as significant as its content. She is motivated by gratitude. She is grateful to a generous nation that saved her from Nazi tyranny and then provided a home for her. She is grateful to the teachers who educated her children and grandchildren. She is grateful to the health care professionals who care for the suffering. Her gratitude takes the form of pride in being American.

She suggests that indulging in cynicism or anger towards one's fellow citizens is to betray one's birthright of freedom.

If anyone has a right to be angry and cynical, it is Ms. Klein. But if she chooses not to be, what right do the rest of us have to negativity?

When someone asked her how she managed to remain positive after all that she experienced, she had this to say:

"The pain of injury can settle in you either as a heavy stone or as a light. And if it settles in you as a light, it gets stronger, and whenever you encounter injustice you can speak up. When you address the injury done to someone else, not only do you liberate them from their pain, you liberate the pain in yourself as well."

At the same time states like Arizona and Alabama are making it much harder for people to come to the United States, we spend relatively little time talking about the responsibilities of those who already live here. How can our nation develop a sane and fair immigration policy when it does not engage in serious deliberation about the obligations of citizenship?

What are the obligations of citizenship? Here is a start:

1. To be informed.
2. To vote.
3. To educate children.
4. To discover one's talents and use them to help others.
5. To treat everyone with respect and dignity.

Ms. Klein refuses to be drawn into political debates about controversial issues like immigration policy. She understands that issues divide, but ideas unite. So before we can have a reasonable discussion about controversial issues, we need to know the positive ideals that give us common ground.

It's a matter of first things first. We need to get over the petty minded thinking that every decision produces winners and losers. By refusing to accept a political mindset that separates all participants into opposing teams before a topic is even discussed, we may recover an America worthy of those who have sacrificed to defend our freedoms.

October 23, 2011

89. MARTIN LUTHER KING, JR.

With a permanent marker I carefully traced out a large number 88 on the back of a white cotton t-shirt, then wrote the name "PAGE" above the numbers. It was 1968. I was six years old, and my hero was Alan Page, defensive end for the Minnesota Vikings.

Putting on the shirt, I walked down the stairs into the living room where family members had gathered to watch Sunday football. I turned my back to the TV watchers, showing off my new "jersey."

"Alan Page?" my uncle laughed. "Don't you know he's black?"

I turned around. All the men were laughing. I ran back upstairs, took off the shirt and never wore it again.

Children are not born into racism, they are mentored in it. Racism is as unpleasant to them as the taste of coffee or cigarettes, and yet for many it comes to feel natural, as the way things are supposed to be, as the way things have always been, and always will be.

1968 was the year Martin Luther King, Jr. was assassinated, standing on the balcony of the Lorraine Motel in Memphis, four years after passage of the Civil Rights Act.

In 1983 President Ronald Reagan signed a bill establishing the third Monday in January as a national holiday in honor of Martin Luther King, Jr. The first official observance of the holiday took place January 20, 1986.

And now, 43 years after King's assassination, few would laugh at a white child wearing a Donald Driver or Adrian Peterson jersey. It's not the most important measure of King's contribution to society, but it is significant. At least in some contexts, people are not "judged by the color of their skin but by the content of their character."

But as our society makes slow, incremental progress toward racial equality, King's relevance seems diminished, not enhanced. That's the downside of making him into an icon. The symbol becomes bigger than the person. If only we would take time to read his essays and speeches, we would discover someone whose wisdom and courage are sorely needed today.

King's commitment to racial justice was grounded in a deep and abiding commitment to goodness. Isn't that what we want from our leaders?

Reading his words now is like taking a deep breath of clean fresh air.

On Political Crisis: Today's problems are so acute because the tragic evasion and defaults of several centuries have accumulated to disaster proportions. The luxury of a leisurely approach to urgent solutions—the ease of gradualism—was forfeited by ignoring the issues for too long.

On Materialism: We must work passionately and indefatigably to bridge the gulf between our scientific progress and our moral progress. One of the great problems of mankind is that we suffer from a poverty of the spirit which stands in glaring contrast to our scientific and technological abundance. The richer we have become materially, the poorer we have become morally and spiritually.

On Corruption: When a culture begins to feel threatened by its own inadequacies, the majority of men tend to prop themselves up by artificial means, rather than dig down deep into their spiritual and cultural wellsprings.

On Leadership: Everybody can be great. Because anybody can serve. You don't have to have a college degree to serve. You don't have to make your subject and your verb agree to serve. You don't have to know about Plato and Aristotle to serve. You don't have to know Einstein's theory of relativity to serve. You don't have to know the second theory of thermodynamics in physics to serve. You only need a heart full of grace. A soul generated by love.

On Democracy: When an individual is no longer a true participant, when he no longer feels a sense of responsibility to his society, the content of democracy is emptied.

King lived to see President Lyndon B. Johnson sign the Civil Rights Act into law. But he did not live to see the end of racial prejudice, class inequality, militaristic aggression, or political corruption—nor will we in our lifetimes. And for that reason, he still has something important to say to us.

January 15, 2012

The Greenleaf Center for Servant Leadership held its 21st annual international conference last week in Dallas. Over 600 people attended from throughout the United States and abroad. What started out in the 1970s as a revolutionary (and quirky) idea has grown steadily into a worldwide movement.

The phrase "servant leadership" was coined 40 years ago by Robert K. Greenleaf in a brief essay entitled "The Servant as Leader." In that essay he articulated a vision that continues to inspire people today: the best leaders are those who have a deep personal commitment to the common good, and out of that commitment comes the desire to lead. What this means is that leadership cannot be defined in terms of style, or technique, or authority; it is primarily a matter of attitude, originating in love and culminating in effective action.

The dominant conception of leadership in our society is the ability to effectively wield power or authority. Most leadership books focus on techniques that enable one to "get ahead" in the race with competing individuals and organizations.

Greenleaf didn't see things that way. He thought of leadership as an obligation to improve people's lives through effective service. Thus, he said, the leader should ask herself: "do those served grow as persons; do they, while being served, become healthier, wiser, freer, more autonomous, more likely themselves to become servants? And, what is the effect on the least privileged in society; will he benefit, or, at least, will he not be further deprived?"

When Greenleaf retired from his 38-year career with AT&T, he founded the Center for Applied Ethics in order to help organizations become more effective. He understood that institutions had become more and more influential in society and that the way to make society better was to work through them. "Whereas, until recently, caring was largely person to person, now most of it is mediated through institutions—often large, complex, powerful, impersonal; not always competent; sometimes corrupt. If a better society is to be built, one that is more just and more loving, one that provides greater creative opportunity for its people, then the most open course is to raise both the capacity to serve and the very performance as servant of existing major institutions by new regenerative forces operating within them."

Over the years, more and more companies have committed to servant leadership and improved themselves and the communities in which they reside as a result. Every year *Fortune* magazine's list of the 100 Best Companies to Work For is dominated by servant-led organizations like W.L. Gore & Associates, SAS, Synovus Financial, S.C. Johnson, and FedEx.

Greenleaf was what I like to think of as a "pragmatic idealist." He knew that there would always be people in power who have little interest in the good for others, whose primary motivations are prestige and self-advancement. To such people, the idea of servant leadership is foolish or perhaps even threatening. But he also knew that there are a certain number of people for whom the idea of serving others resonates deeply, and that they need to be encouraged to take more responsibility—to speak up at meetings, to run for public office, to resist the temptation to "go along to get along."

Six-hundred people attending a conference are not going to change the world. But that's okay. The people I talked to last week in Dallas weren't there because they wanted to change the whole world. They just wanted to be more effective at changing their little corner of the world. And that's how big changes always start.

June 19, 2011